YOUNG READERS' EDITION

NOTORIOUS
RBG

THE LIFE AND TIMES OF
RUTH BADER GINSBURG

YOUNG READERS' EDITION

NOTORIOUS
RBG

THE LIFE AND TIMES OF
RUTH BADER GINSBURG

IRIN CARMON & SHANA KNIZHNIK

WITH KATHLEEN KRULL

HARPER

An Imprint of HarperCollinsPublishers

Notorious RBG: The Life and Times of Ruth Bader Ginsburg Young Readers' Edition

Library of Congress Control Number: 2017949440
ISBN 978-0-06-274853-9

Typography by Torborg Davern
 19 20 21   PC/LSCC   10 9 8 7 6 5 4 3 2

First Edition

To the women on whose shoulders we stand

Contents

1

A Supreme Inspiration

Sometimes a necklace is more than just a necklace. If you're Supreme Court Justice Ruth Bader Ginsburg of the United States Supreme Court—someone who has a lot to say—even what you wear around your neck sends a message. When it's the end of June and everyone is breathlessly waiting for the Supreme Court to hand down its most important decisions, those lacey or sparkly collars over her black robe, called jabots, are a clue to what's about to happen.

On June 25, 2013, Justice Ginsburg, nicknamed RBG, took her seat on the curved Supreme Court bench wearing a spiky jabot with scalloped glass beads. It's a necklace she only brings out when she has to, and that day her message was loud and clear. *I dissent.*

The math of the Supreme Court is pretty simple. Nine: that's how many justices there (usually) are, picked by a president to serve for life or as long as the justice wants. Four: that's how many justices have to agree to take a case, since they get asked to decide thousands of disputes and can take fewer than one hundred. Five: that's how many justices need to agree on a result. And then at least one of the majority needs to explain, in writing, *why*. After all, they say what the law means for the entire country, and everyone, including the president, Congress, and judges across America, is supposed to follow.

But let's say one of the justices thinks the five or more in the majority are wrong. She or he doesn't have to clam up and take it. That's when she can publicly push back in a written dissent, to tell the world how *she* thinks the case should have gone. And if she's feeling particularly salty, the justice can sit in the courtroom when the majority announces its opinion and tell the world exactly how she feels. The Supreme Court is a pretty polite place, so it doesn't happen a lot.

RBG was feeling particularly salty that week.

After twenty years as a Supreme Court justice, the eighty-year-old was about to break a record by dissenting from the bench: publicly and verbally demanding her colleagues and the world listen to her protest. That's how bad she believed matters had gotten.

That day, five justices, led by Chief Justice John Roberts, had decided the country no longer needed an important part of a law known as the Voting Rights Act. The law, first passed by Congress in 1965, acknowledged an ugly truth. State governments, which create many voting rules, had been coming up with all kinds of ways to block African Americans from voting. Thanks to the Voting Rights Act, states that had a track record of discrimination had to ask the federal government for permission to change their voting laws so the government could decide whether those laws hurt historically oppressed people.

But no more. "Any racial discrimination in voting is too much," Roberts declared that morning. "But our country has changed in the last fifty years." He pointed out that America had elected the first black president in 2008. Roberts said his piece, then added, evenly, "Justice Ginsburg has filed a dissenting opinion."

A woman who defies stereotypes, RBG has survived sorrows and setbacks, always beating the strong odds against her. Fierce and knowing, she does not mess around, and you don't want to mess with her. But even after she had spent years as one of the most important judges in the country, some people assume they can count her out because she is small and delicate and has survived cancer twice. But on that morning, there was no mistaking her passion.

At stake, RBG told the courtroom, was "what was once the subject of a dream, the equal citizenship stature of all in our polity, a voice to every voter in our democracy undiluted by race." It was an obvious reference to Martin Luther King Jr.'s famous "I Have a

Dream" speech, but the phrase "equal citizenship stature"—meaning everyone is treated equally under the law—had special meaning to RBG in particular.

Forty years ago, she had stood before this very bench, as a young lawyer before nine male justices, and forced them to see that women were people too in the eyes of the Constitution. That women, along with men, deserved equality, to stand with all the rights and responsibilities that being a citizen meant. As part of a global movement for women's rights, RBG had gone from facing closed doors to winning five out of six of the women's rights cases she argued before the Supreme Court.

No one—not the firms and judges that had refused to hire her because she was a young mother, not the bosses who had paid her less for being a woman—had ever expected her to be sitting up there at the court.

At nearly ten thirty a.m. that day in June, RBG quoted Martin Luther King Jr. directly: "The arc of the moral universe is long, but it bends towards justice," she said. But then she added her own words: "if there is a steadfast commitment to see the task through to completion." Not exactly poetry. But pure RBG. She has always been steadfast, and when the work is justice, she has every intention to see it to the end.

In her written dissent, RBG had a snappy way of explaining what made no sense about the majority's opinion. They were killing the Voting Rights Act because it had *worked too well*. That, she wrote, was like "throwing away your umbrella in a rainstorm because you are not getting wet."

Although three of her colleagues agreed with her, she couldn't get one more to make a majority. But all was not lost, because the country was listening, and they were inspired.

In Washington, D.C., two friends, Aminatou Sow and Frank Chi, plastered the city with stickers of RBG's image, giving the justice an illustrated crown inspired by the artist Jean-Michel Basquiat and a caption: "Can't spell truth without Ruth." In Cambridge, Massachusetts, twenty-six-year-old law student Hallie Jay Pope started drawing comics of RBG, made an "I Heart RBG" shirt, and donated the proceeds to a voting rights organization. And in New York, twenty-four-year-old NYU law student Shana Knizhnik, one of the authors of this book, was aghast at the gutting of voting rights. She tried to look on the bright side: at least Justice Ginsburg was speaking up. On Facebook, Shana's friend gave the justice a nickname: Notorious RBG. Inspired, Shana took to Tumblr to create a tribute.

It started as kind of a joke, the reference to the three-hundred-pound deceased rapper Notorious B.I.G. After all, what did an eighty-year-old Jewish lady have in common with a nineties gangsta rapper? But there were similarities. They were both from Brooklyn. And like her namesake, B.I.G., this jurist who demanded patience as she spoke could also pack a verbal punch.

You could say the Notorious RBG meme took off from there. RBG, already a hero to people who knew about the law and women's rights, was suddenly being celebrated in all kinds of places you don't usually hear about the Supreme Court. She was on mugs and even tattoos. (For the record, the tattoos kind of freak her out. She's still a Jewish grandma.)

Her family, while amused, was also a little surprised at this late-in-life turn to megafame. "I would not have thought of her as hip," says her son, James.

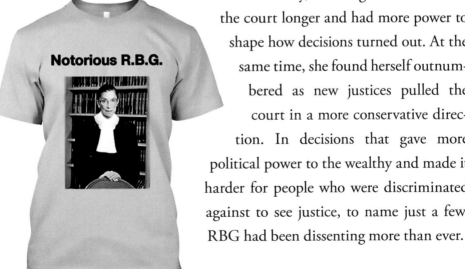

Why now? Well, RBG's position on the court had changed. She had more seniority, meaning she had been on the court longer and had more power to shape how decisions turned out. At the same time, she found herself outnumbered as new justices pulled the court in a more conservative direction. In decisions that gave more political power to the wealthy and made it harder for people who were discriminated against to see justice, to name just a few, RBG had been dissenting more than ever.

Can you believe this firebrand once had a reputation for being shy and trying to make things work? And yet even when she chose to use her voice more softly, RBG has never been one to shrink from a challenge. People who think she is hanging on to this world by a thread underestimate her. RBG's main concession to hitting her late seventies was to give up water-skiing.

But don't worry, she's still keeping herself in fighting shape. In late November 2014, RBG felt a little faint during a workout session with her regular personal trainer and had to have heart surgery. Still, she had court arguments to attend and plans to keep. "I would be glad to greet the clever creators of the Notorious R.B.G. in chambers," she had written to them. (*Chambers* is what the justices call their offices.)

So on a December morning, RBG stood, flanked by her clerks, ready to greet the creators of Notorious RBG and Can't Spell Truth without Ruth. Her slender wrist was still slightly bruised from the surgical procedure.

Her guests asked her what message she had for all the young people who admired her. RBG paused to think it over. "You can tell them," she replied, "I'll be back doing push-ups next week."

Nine Things to Know about the Supreme Court of the United States (SCOTUS)

1. The Supreme Court is the highest court in the land, the place of last resort. It reviews and can overturn decisions by the lower courts.

2. It was men only for two centuries until Sandra Day O'Connor was appointed in 1981. RBG, the second woman to join SCOTUS, was appointed in 1993.

3. Getting to be a justice—a chief justice or one of the eight associate justices—is a long, hard road.

4. Justices are appointed for life, serving on the court until they die or decide to retire.

5. As soon as one justice exits, the president nominates a new justice and asks the Senate to confirm her or him.

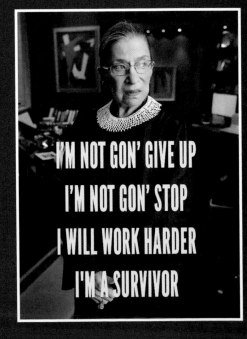

I'M NOT GON' GIVE UP

I'M NOT GON' STOP

I WILL WORK HARDER

I'M A SURVIVOR

6. SCOTUS starts its term every year on the first Monday of October, hearing cases, doing heavy-duty research, and arguing like mad until June or July, when it delivers its verdicts.

7. SCOTUS is picky—it takes only about seventy-five cases a year out of the seven thousand it is asked to hear. It looks for the cases where other judges have disagreed about what the law means, especially ones that raise the most significant issues relating to the US Constitution.

8. Its decisions, which are explained in written opinions, can be controversial.

9. The court affects the daily lives of every American, from how police interact with people to how schools treat students.

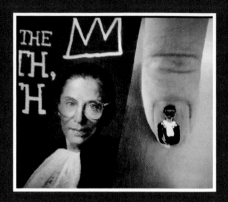

Ruth Bader Ginsburg
Herstory in the making!

Been in This Game for Years

July 19–20, 1848

"We hold these truths to be self-evident: that all men and women are created equal."

—Declaration of Sentiments at Seneca Falls at the first women's rights convention

1820   1830   1840

1828: Supreme Court justices bunk together, until one woman ruins it for everyone by insisting on living with her husband.

December 1853

"Was invited to sit in the Chief Justice's seat. As I took the place, I involuntarily exclaimed: 'Who knows, but this chair may one day be occupied by a woman.' The brethren laughed heartily."

—abolitionist feminist Sarah Grimké

1850   1860   1870   1880   1890   1900

July 28, 1868: The Fourteenth Amendment to the Constitution recognizes the citizenship rights of ex-slaves and promises equal protection under the law, but makes it clear that only men's voting rights count. (And even that much remains a promise on paper.)

April 15, 1873: The Supreme Court allows Illinois to block Myra Bradwell from practicing law because she's a woman.

"The paramount destiny and mission of women are to fulfill the noble and benign offices of wife and mother. This is the law of the Creator."

—Justice Joseph P. Bradley, in a concurrence in *Bradwell v. Illinois*

August 18, 1920: The Nineteenth Amendment recognizes women's right to vote, though high barriers remain for women of color.

June 10, 1932: Martin D. Ginsburg, future husband of RBG, is born.

| 1900 | 1910 | 1920 | 1930 | 1940 |

1903: Celia Amster, RBG's mother, is born.

March 15, 1933: Joan Ruth Bader, nicknamed Kiki, is born in Brooklyn.

1944: Lucile Lomen becomes the first female clerk at the Supreme Court.

June 1950: Celia Bader dies one day before her daughter's high school graduation.

1953: Simone de Beauvoir's *The Second Sex*, a major influence on the upcoming women's movement, is published in the United States.

July 21, 1955: RBG's daughter, Jane Ginsburg, is born.

1958: Marty graduates from Harvard Law School and they move to New York City, where a good job awaits him. RBG transfers to Columbia Law School.

1959: RBG graduates from Columbia Law at the top of her class but can barely get a job.

1950

1960

Fall 1950: RBG enrolls at Cornell.

June 1954: Ruth Bader graduates from Cornell. She marries Marty at his family's home.

1956: RBG enrolls in Harvard Law School, one of only nine women in her class. In her second year, Marty is diagnosed with cancer.

1961: The Supreme Court okays making jury duty for women optional because "woman is still regarded as the center of home and family life."

HARPER'S WEEKLY

"NOT GUILTY!"—ON ACCOUNT OF HIS GOOD LOOKS

1963: President John F. Kennedy signs the Equal Pay Act, which bans discrimination in pay on the basis of sex. It's full of exceptions.

1967: President Johnson nominates famed civil rights litigator Thurgood Marshall (and RBG inspiration) to be the first black justice on the Supreme Court.

1965: RBG publishes her first book, *Civil Procedure in Sweden*.

1960   1970

1962: Civil rights activist and visionary legal scholar Pauli Murray proposes using the Fourteenth Amendment to argue against sexist laws.

September 8, 1965: RBG's son, James Ginsburg, is born.

1964: President Lyndon B. Johnson signs into law the Civil Rights Act of 1964, which contains a last-minute ban on sex discrimination in employment.

1963: RBG becomes the second woman to teach full-time at Rutgers School of Law.

1972: Richard Nixon signs into law Title IX, which bans sex discrimination in education.

1971: RBG writes her first brief, or written argument, to the Supreme Court in *Reed v. Reed.*

1974: RBG publishes the first-ever casebook on sex discrimination. She insists that the authors' names be listed alphabetically, even though doing so means the one man's name will come first.

1970

1980

1972: RBG becomes the first female tenured professor at Columbia Law School.

1970: While at Rutgers, RBG teaches her first class on women and the law.

1972: RBG cofounds the Women's Rights Project at the American Civil Liberties Union.

1980: President Jimmy Carter nominates RBG to the United States Court of Appeals for the District of Columbia Circuit.

2000: RBG is one of four dissenters in *Bush v. Gore*, which effectively declares George W. Bush president.

1993: President Bill Clinton nominates RBG to be a justice and the second woman on the Supreme Court.

1996: RBG writes the majority opinion in the landmark case *United States v. Virginia*, requiring the Virginia Military Institute to admit women.

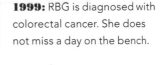

1990

2000

1999: RBG is diagnosed with colorectal cancer. She does not miss a day on the bench.

1981: President Ronald Reagan nominates Sandra Day O'Connor to be the first woman on the Supreme Court. Two of the male justices had previously suggested they would resign if a woman ever joined their ranks, but they stay put.

2005: Sandra Day O'Connor announces her retirement.

"To my sorrow, I am now what [O'Connor] was her first twelve years on the court—the lone woman."

—RBG

2009: President Barack Obama nominates Federal Appeals Court Judge Sonia Sotomayor to the Supreme Court. She is the first Latina justice.

"I like the idea that we're all over the bench. It says women are here to stay."

—RBG

2007: RBG reads her dissent from the bench in the sex discrimination case of Lilly Ledbetter.

February 5, 2009: RBG has pancreatic cancer surgery.

2000

2010

February 23, 2009: RBG is back on the bench.

"I wanted people to see that the Supreme Court isn't all male."

—RBG

2009: RBG attends President Obama's first speech to Congress.

"I don't know. I hear that Justice Ginsburg has been working on her jump shot."

—Barack Obama, after being invited to play basketball at the nation's highest court

June 25, 2013: RBG dissents from the bench (one of her five oral dissents that year) in a case gutting the Voting Rights Act.

June 27, 2010: Marty Ginsburg dies after complications from cancer.

2013: Notorious R.B.G., the Tumblr, is born.

2010

2020

August 2013: RBG becomes the first Supreme Court justice to officiate at a same-sex wedding.

2010: President Obama nominates Solicitor General Elena Kagan to the Supreme Court.

2

A Girl Who Could Think for Herself

*B*aby Ruth was born in 1933 in Brooklyn, New York, to proud parents Celia and Nathan Bader. She had an older sister, Marilyn, who nicknamed her Kiki.

Alas, Ruth lost one of them when she was still a toddler. Her sister, Marilyn, died of meningitis, a painful—and at the time deadly—inflammation. She was only six.

Celia poured her hopes and dreams into her daughter Ruth. Her fondest wish was that Ruth would be able to achieve things she hadn't been allowed to do herself.

When Celia was young, she had shown great promise, graduating from high school with top grades at age fifteen. But Celia was born in

1903 and in her day girls didn't go on to higher education. Instead, she had helped put someone *else* through college—a boy (her brother).

Celia went to work as a bookkeeper in Manhattan's garment district, the center for fashion design and manufacturing. Dutifully she turned her earnings over to her family.

Then she married Nathan, Ruth's dad, who worked in the fur trade. With furs being a luxury item, his business was not doing particularly well during the Great Depression, when most people were struggling.

As soon as she got married, Celia quit her job. To work outside the home was to have people think her husband couldn't support her. That was the way things were then, not that Celia ever necessarily agreed with "the way things were."

Even as a little girl, Ruth could sense her mother's disappointment in life, the pang of her thwarted ambitions. Celia had loved to learn, and could have had a successful career—or at least a job. But doors for women were closed, and few were doing much to open them.

In Ruth's neighborhood, the paths for boys and girls were clear: sons were to become doctors or lawyers, and "the girls were supposed to marry doctors or lawyers," according to one of Ruth's classmates.

Celia, on the other hand, wanted to push Ruth to follow her own path, a path that would be just right for Ruth.

THE POWER OF NANCY DREW

It wasn't long before Ruth was devouring books. From their house on East Ninth Street, Celia walked her to the local library once a week. While her mom got her hair done at the salon, Ruth picked out five books at a time. From an interest in mythology she moved on to Nancy Drew mysteries: "This was a girl who was an adventurer," she said later, "who could think for herself, who was the dominant person in her relationship with her young boyfriend."

A strong girl who could think for herself—that sounded like a goal.

Ruth treasured her weekly adventures, a special mother-daughter time. The library was one floor above a Chinese restaurant: "I learned to love the smell of Chinese food in those days," she remembered fondly.

From her Irish, Polish, and Italian neighbors, Ruth sometimes encountered anti-Jewish prejudice. She never forgot one hurtful sign: *No Dogs or Jews Allowed*. Children couldn't help hearing their parents whisper about what was going on in Europe—the Holocaust, in which six million Jews were killed.

Compared to Europe, Brooklyn seemed a safe place to grow up. Ruth had mostly happy memories of her childhood—riding her bike to school, learning new things, playing with cousins and friends.

One of her earliest interests was music. When she was eleven, she saw a stirring performance of an opera. Instantly, Ruth decided she wanted to be a singer. Unfortunately, she said, "I am a monotone." No one encouraged her, either: "My grade school teachers were cruel. They rated me a sparrow, not a robin."

But there was plenty she was good at.

Quiet but popular, Ruth made a splash when she got to high school. She earned excellent grades—once she showed her mom a report card that was less than perfect, and that was the last time *that* happened. And she whirled her way through activities. She played cello in the orchestra, wrote for the school newspaper, and served as treasurer of the Go-Getters cheerleading club. She was high-energy—at halftime she twirled her baton so vigorously that she once chipped a tooth with it.

In the summers, she journeyed to leafy Upstate New York, to a camp for Jewish children in the Adirondack Mountains. Showing a gift for leadership, she was named camp rabbi, its religious leader (at a time when there were no women rabbis in real life).

Fifteen-year-old RBG as camp rabbi at Che-Na-Wah in the Adirondacks

She also met a nice boy headed for law school. He became her boyfriend.

Ruth was always curious. At Passover seders—the festive meal recounting the Jews' exodus from Egypt—she was the one who asked the most questions. But, like all Jewish girls at the time, she wasn't allowed to join the boys studying for their bar mitzvahs, the coming-of-age ritual. The bat mitzvah, the Jewish ceremony for girls, was rarely performed then, and it wouldn't have occurred to Ruth to ask for one.

NO ORDINARY MOM

Part of Ruth's childhood ended when she turned thirteen. Her mother was struck with cancer, and it became clear that Celia wasn't going to survive.

Later, Ruth described her house as having the smell of death. But at the time, she told no one what was happening, not wanting people to pity her. Dealing with death at such a young age was overwhelming.

Trying to keep her mom's spirits up, Ruth did her homework every night at Celia's bedside. Ruth would treasure her mother's words for years to come:

★ *Always be a lady: "That meant always conduct yourself civilly, don't let emotions like anger or envy get in your way. . . . Don't snap back in anger. Anger, resentment, indulgence in recriminations waste time and sap energy."*

★ *"Hold fast to your convictions and your self-respect."*

★ *Last but definitely not least: always be independent.*

These were *not* the typical lessons that typical moms were passing on to daughters in those days—especially that last one. Even then Ruth seemed to realize that her mom was unusual, a source of strength not all girls were lucky enough to have.

No one impacted Ruth more than her mom.

By the time Ruth graduated from James Madison High School, her name peppered the graduation program, with multiple awards and honors.

RUTH BADER
1584 East 9th Street
Arista, Treas. of Go-Getters, School Orchestra, Twirlers, Sec. to English Department Chairman, Feature Editor Term Newspaper
Cornell University

Just Some of the Things Women Couldn't Do in the 1930s and 1940s

★ Practice law in most states, much less become a judge

★ Get paid the same amount as men for doing the same work

★ Answer want ads for jobs labeled "men only"

★ Attend most Ivy League universities

★ Serve on a jury in most states

★ Play school sports on an equal basis with boys

★ Open a bank account or get a credit card without a husband's or male relative's permission

★ Attend a military academy

★ Become an astronaut

★ Get pregnant without the real threat of losing her job

★ In some states, own property without having a husband in sole control as "head and master"

★ Wear pants on the US Senate floor

★ Serve in combat in the military

On the much-anticipated day of the ceremony, she should have been at school, happily accepting her awards while her parents beamed.

Instead she was absent, home with her father.

Her beloved mom had died the day before, at age forty-seven. It broke Ruth's heart that Celia hadn't lived long enough to see her daughter on her big day.

Ruth was submerged in sadness as their house filled up with mourning women. None of them—much less a girl like Ruth—was allowed to be in the minyan, the quorum of adults needed for prayer under Jewish law. All she could do was try to help her father and grieve in silence.

ON HER WAY UP

Ruth's high school yearbook predicted that one particular senior would go all the way to the top and become a Supreme Court justice.

The senior wasn't Ruth, though. In 1950, the idea of a woman on the Supreme Court was supremely laughable.

No, it was a classmate named Joel . . . who went on to become a perfectly respectable dentist.

With her stellar grades and impressive roster of activities, Ruth was proud to be headed to prestigious Cornell University. Cornell was one of the few Ivy League universities that would accept women. And in one of her last acts to help her daughter, Celia had managed to scrape together eight thousand dollars to help with college expenses.

"It was one of the most trying times in my life," Ruth said of the painful period following her mom's death. But the grief seemed to give her a focus, to fine-tune her goals: "I knew that she wanted me to study hard and get good grades and succeed in life.

"So that's what I did."

Ruth Bader was already on her own path, on her way to becoming the glorious and notorious RBG.

3

You Could Drop a Bomb over Her Head

In 1950, when Ruth arrived at Cornell to study, everyone assumed women came to college for one reason: to husband hunt. And Cornell University in Ithaca, New York, seemed—to parents and daughters alike—to be pretty good hunting grounds. After all, the ratio of men to women was four to one.

That also meant, of course, that the competition was intense to be admitted to one of the few spots reserved for women. As Ruth later remarked wryly, "The women were a heck of a lot smarter than the men."

This was also an era when women were supposed to hide their smarts. Girls and women were told not to look too brainy, for fear of scaring off a potential husband. Ruth didn't come to Cornell to find a man, but she wasn't interested in broadcasting her seriousness. So she created a mental map of every women's bathroom on campus. These became her safe places to study. She would take a bag of books and stay in the lounge area until her homework was done. (The bathroom in the architecture school, she decided, was the best.)

Her dorm room was located in a corridor with six other Jewish girls who had come from big cities like her. After the ten p.m. curfew, the other girls would play bridge, but Ruth would just keep on working. Said one roommate: "You could drop a bomb over her head and she wouldn't know it."

NOT A TOTAL NERD

As intense as Ruth was, she did have a social life. She joined a sorority, and she kept up with her boyfriend from summer camp. He went to Columbia Law School, and she saw him on weekends.

But classes always came first, and there were so many that grabbed her attention. Her mom had wanted her to become a teacher—that was a solid job for a woman. So Ruth tried education classes and student teaching, but she soon realized her interests were elsewhere.

She was much more intrigued in her European literature class. The professor was the well-known Russian writer Vladimir Nabokov, and he ended up being one of her biggest influences. He was the one who taught her the importance of writing well, of thinking carefully about where each and every word should go.

RBG

The Alpha Epsilon Phi sorority at Cornell in 1953

A NEW GOAL

She also loved a class in constitutional law that was taught by a famous professor, Robert Cushman. She began working as a research assistant to him, helping him to put together an exhibition on book burning, which was an extreme example of censorship.

She was fascinated by history and current events. The segregation of African Americans dismayed her. World War II, which she later called "a war against racism," had ended five years earlier, yet it was a war that had involved racism on America's part. "I came to understand that our troops in that war were separated by race, until the end. There was something wrong about that."

While Ruth was at Cornell, a senator named Joseph McCarthy was starting to get national attention. His committee was investigating all sorts of people—including a Cornell zoology professor. McCarthy suspected many citizens of sympathizing with communism, a system of government in which all property is held in common. The Soviet Union was a communist country, at least in theory, and during the 1950s, it was considered America's biggest enemy. McCarthy conducted cruel, often baseless investigations into potential communist traitors to the United States—investigations that ruined lives and careers. Lawyers were the ones who stood up to him, showing how he was jeopardizing crucial American ideals, like freedom of thought and speech.

"I got the idea," said Ruth, "that being a lawyer was a pretty good thing, because in addition to practicing a profession, you could do something good for your society."

Her father, Nathan, was worried. There were hardly any women lawyers. Getting a job would be impossible. How was she going to be able to support herself? Her goal seemed totally unrealistic.

By Ruth's senior year of college, her father was relieved that Ruth, without even particularly trying, had fallen in love with a guy who looked like he was going to be able to support her. Problem solved. That's not how Ruth saw her relationship, though.

She was just thrilled that she'd finally met a boy who cared that she had a brain.

ENTER MARTY

Her relationship with Martin Ginsburg, a chemistry major one year ahead of her at Cornell, didn't start out as a romance.

The boyfriend of one of Ruth's roommates was friends with Marty—a funny, confident guy who drove a gray Chevy. They introduced him to Ruth in the hopes of creating a foursome who could all hang out together. Marty had a girlfriend at another college, and Ruth still had her boyfriend at Columbia. They were just friends.

He seemed to have made up his mind to be more than that before she did: "I have no doubt that in our case I liked her more first," he later recalled.

But Ruth began to reconsider, especially in the lonely winter: "There was a long, cold week at Cornell. So that's how we started." She soon had a news flash. "It occurred to me that Martin D. Ginsburg was ever so much smarter than my boyfriend at Columbia Law School."

As one of Marty's best friends saw the courtship, "Ruth was a wonderful student and a beautiful young woman. Most of the men were in awe of her, but Marty was not. He's never been in awe of anybody. He wooed and won her by convincing her how much he respected her."

It helped that Ruth really liked his parents too and enjoyed her visits to the Ginsburg home on Long Island. Marty's father was the vice president of a chain of department stores (Ruth worked one summer at one of his stores), and his mother was delighted to take Ruth under her wing, becoming a motherly figure.

FIRST IN HER CLASS

Marty was different from the other boys: he assumed that Ruth would have a career. He hoped they could go on to study together at Harvard University in Cambridge, Massachusetts. The couple wanted "to be in the same discipline so there would be something you could talk about, bounce ideas off of, know what each other was doing." He added, "We actually sat down and by process of elimination came up with the law."

Marty had dropped his chemistry major—it interfered with his golf practice—so that ruled out medical school. There was business school, but Harvard Business School didn't accept women. Marty later realized that only he had needed to make up his mind to study law: "I have thought deep in my heart that Ruth always intended that to be the case," he said years later.

They both got into Harvard Law School, which had started accepting women four years earlier. Marty dove into law while Ruth finished up her final year at Cornell.

All her hours of studying in the bathroom paid off, and she graduated at the top of her class with a bachelor's degree in government.

In June 1954, days after her graduation, she married Marty in the Ginsburgs' living room with eighteen people present. In Judaism that number symbolizes life.

Just before the ceremony, Marty's mother called her aside to give her a surprising little gift: a pair of earplugs. "I'm going to tell you the secret of a happy marriage," she said, by way of explanation: "It sometimes helps to be a little deaf."

What did that mean?

At some point, during her honeymoon in Europe, Ruth realized what her mother-in-law meant: "Sometimes people say unkind or thoughtless things, and when they do, it is best to be a little hard of hearing—to tune out and not snap back in anger or impatience." The words echoed advice from Ruth's own mom, and she took them to heart. The advice would come in handy far beyond her marriage.

A DETOUR

Before the couple could forge ahead at Harvard, Marty was called to military duty—serving two years teaching at the artillery school at the Fort Sill army base in Oklahoma.

Ruth went to work as a secretary in a law firm, but she was a terrible typist. She took the civil service exam to work for the federal government—and got a bitter lesson in discrimination and the unfairness of petty bureaucracy.

Workers were classified according to a general schedule (GS) of earnings and responsibility. Ruth was classified GS-5, until she made the "mistake" of mentioning that she was three months pregnant. Her rank promptly dropped to GS-2: less money and less responsibility. Another army wife

The newlyweds at Fort Sill, Oklahoma, in fall 1954

was pregnant too, but wisely told no one until she had to—and then was expected to quit immediately, before she gave birth. It was perfectly legal to demote or fire women for being pregnant.

In retrospect, the two years the couple spent together in Oklahoma, far from everything and everyone they knew, supplied a sturdy start to their partnership. Marty acknowledged that it allowed the two "to learn about each other and begin to build a life." Neither of their jobs were particularly demanding. For the first (and last) time in their lives, they had the luxury of lots of free time to spend together.

They borrowed books and opera records from the library on base, and whenever New York's Metropolitan Opera traveling company came to Dallas, they'd drive three hours to see the performance. Ruth still loved to sing—"but only in the shower."

They split the housework, not exactly down the middle, but "doing whatever you did a little better or liked a little more or disliked less," said Marty. Without bickering, they made it work.

THE TuNA-CASSEROLE iNCiDENT

There was one thing Marty did a *lot* better.

One night, shortly after their wedding, Ruth, trying to do her housewifely duty, presented him with dinner.

"What is it?" he asked, squinting at the lumpy mess.

A tuna casserole, she assured him.

The meal inspired him to learn how to cook. He began working his way through a fancy French cookbook—not the normal fare on an army base—finding that his chemistry skills still came in handy.

Marty's specialty was more formal-occasion food, while Ruth (reluctantly) handled the daily cooking—for the time being. Thawing a frozen vegetable and some meat usually did the trick: "I had seven things I could make, and when we got to number seven, we went back to number one."

They welcomed their first child, Jane, in 1955.

The officers' nursery started taking babies when they were two months old, and it was open until midnight.

Marty had read that the first year of a child's life is when the personality forms, and he threw himself into taking care of Jane. He played classical music for her and took over the two a.m. feeding, because it was easier for him to fall back asleep than it was for Ruth.

It was looking ahead to Harvard that made the new mom panic—far less support, far more demands. Her father-in-law came to her rescue. First, when Harvard took away her scholarship because now she had a husband with a wealthy family, he paid her expensive tuition. Then he gave her a little pep talk: "Ruth, if you don't want to go to law school you have the best reason in the world and no one would think less of you. But if you really want to go to law school, you will stop feeling sorry for yourself. You will find a way."

Ruth really wanted to go to law school—and she would find a way.

SOMETHING STRANGE AND SINGULAR

Not that it would come easy. Law school was a lot of work, and for women there was *no* guarantee of a job afterward. Refusing to hire women was perfectly legal. But law school was her *dream*.

As Ruth put it, "The study of the law was unusual for women of my generation. For most girls growing up in the 1940s, the most important degree was not your B.A., but your M.R.S." That was the joke back then—that what mattered wasn't a bachelor of arts degree, but becoming Mrs. Somebody.

In law school Ruth found herself even more outnumbered than at Cornell—five hundred men, nine very smart women. It made her uncomfortable. She felt that she and the other women were like animals being gawked at in a zoo. They were "something strange and singular."

The pressure was intense: "You felt in class as if all eyes were on you and that if you didn't perform well, you would be failing not only for yourself, but for all women." Some professors even held Ladies' Day, when they would call only on the women, with humiliating questions.

One night in 1956, the dean of the law school, Erwin Griswold, invited the nine women over for dinner, along with some important professors Ruth was thrilled to meet. The dean went around the room, asking each woman the same blunt question: How could each of these female students justify being in law school, where they were taking the place of a man?

As the women reddened and shifted in their seats, Ruth wanted to crawl under the couch. No one knew what to say. One woman sassily responded that she was there to find a husband. (She was kidding.) Ruth couldn't summon the wits to come up with her own honest answer, so she mumbled, "I wanted to know more about what my husband does. So that I can be a sympathetic and understanding wife."

She was lying, but no one caught on.

It was embarrassing, but nevertheless she persisted. She worked out a childcare routine, which the family could thankfully afford. She hired a grandmotherly babysitter, who cared for Jane while Ruth attended classes and studied until four p.m. Then she spent hours with Jane until bedtime. The rhythm to her days gave her a balance— the ferocity of brain work relieved by child play.

NO WOMEN ALLOWED

With her perfect grades (surpassing Marty's, as he was fond of bragging), she made it onto the editorial staff of the *Harvard Law Review*, the most prestigious law journal in the country. She was one of only two women who made it on.

Women were finally allowed on the law school campus, but Harvard still put up barriers, real and symbolic. For example, there were no women's bathrooms in one of the two buildings in which classes and exams were held. That meant she had to run across campus just to pee.

One particular evening, still working furiously at midnight, she needed to check a reference in a journal in the Lamont Library reading room. But the Lamont Library reading room didn't allow women to enter its hallowed hall—it even had a guard at the door.

RBG

The men (and two women) of the Harvard Law Review *Board of Editors, 1957–58*

Ruth tried bargaining with the guard, begging him to at least let her stand at the door while *he* grabbed the journal for her. He refused to budge. Ruth had to find another way to complete her assignment.

Having a supportive husband and in-laws was a big help. While other women worried that going to law school would ruin their chances of marriage or that their husbands would disapprove of wives with ambition, Ruth had a husband who boasted that his wife was doing better than him. The only thing he ever teased her about was her driving, and even she had to agree—she had failed her driver's test the first five times she'd taken it.

A NEW SUPERPOWER

A serious blow struck the young family in 1957, when Marty was diagnosed with testicular cancer. He had to undergo radical surgery and daily radiation treatments for six weeks.

Ruth rose to the occasion brilliantly. Besides nursing him, she threw herself into making sure that he kept on track with his studies, corralling the best note takers in his classes to help. She helped Marty in writing his third-year paper until he fell asleep around two a.m. Then she would make the switch to her own work, never missing a beat.

That's how she discovered a sort of superpower: she could get by on one or two hours of sleep a night if she had to, as long as she could sleep in on the weekends.

Against all the odds, and with Ruth's help, Marty survived. He graduated and began working as a tax attorney at a firm in New York City. The family was determined to stick together, and so Ruth transferred from Harvard Law in Cambridge to Columbia Law School in New York.

Her stellar reputation preceded her. "We had heard that the smartest person on the East Coast was going to transfer," said a classmate later, "and that we were all going to drop down one rank."

Marty, Jane, and RBG in summer 1958

Women, of course, had a tough time at Columbia as well. Once a woman began a sentence in class with "I feel," and the professor cut her off with an insult: "Women feel, men think."

Ruth was unperturbed, making the *Law Review* at Columbia too and graduating in 1959—tied for first in her class.

But in 1959, doors all over the place were closed to women.

In other words, what next?

4

Professor RBG

Strange, but true. The supremely qualified Ruth got no job offers once she graduated from law school, even with her most impressive credentials.

The law school posted sign-up sheets for interviews with corporate law firms. Most were labeled "men only." Ruth did manage to snag two interviews, to which she wore her best black suit, but to no avail. She had spent one summer clerking in a New York law firm, which normally would have led to a job, but the firm had already hired a woman that year, and one was enough for them. (The woman was Pauli Murray, who would later have an enormous impact on Ruth.)

As Ruth saw it, she was fighting discrimination on several fronts, with three strikes against her: she was a woman, the mother of a four-year-old, and Jewish. Her situation seemed hopeless.

A FLABBERGASTED JuDGE

One of Ruth's law school professors tried to help out by sending her name to Felix Frankfurter. He was a justice on the US Supreme Court who liked to have Harvard law professors pick his clerks, two of them each term. Clerking was a short-term job, but it meant getting to work closely with the justices to research and draft their opinions. The law-school graduates who snared these positions, nearly always men, went on to the most desired jobs.

When Frankfurter read the name Ruth Bader Ginsburg as a pick for clerk, he was flummoxed. He burst into his chambers and announced to his clerks (all male, of course) that he had unbelievable news. A woman as his clerk! Hilarious!

As it happened, one of the clerks had known Ruth since high school, and he spoke up to support her. Frankfurter shot back that Ruth "had a couple of kids, and her husband has been ill, and you

know that I work you guys very very hard, and I do curse sometimes." (Women were supposed to be too delicate to hear swear words.) He was dredging up every possible excuse, even though most of them weren't true. Ruth had only one child at that time. Around the Supreme

Court, clerking for Frankfurter was considered a cushy job. And he didn't in fact use four-letter words.

Nevertheless, he said no. It was the first time he'd refused a Harvard-approved candidate.

Ruth wasn't all that surprised. She knew about Judge Learned Hand, a Federal Court of Appeals judge she respected, who *did* have a reputation for using profanity. He refused to hire women because he didn't want to have to watch his language around them.

A BIT OF BLACKMAIL

Another professor, Gerald Gunther, came to Ruth's aid, recommending her as a law clerk for Edmund Palmieri, a judge in the Southern District of New York. Palmieri was skeptical—how could a woman with a small child at home be up to this demanding job?

Gunther offered a stick and a carrot: if Palmieri didn't give Ruth a chance, Gunther swore he would never recommend another potential clerk. He also promised Palmieri that if Ruth didn't work out, he would provide the name of a male replacement.

Needless to say, Ruth worked out just fine. More than fine. Palmieri later said that she was one of his best clerks ever. Over the course of two years, she worked even harder than she probably needed to, taking work home and coming in on weekends.

As it happened, Judges Hand and Palmieri lived around the corner from each other, and Palmieri often gave him and Ruth a ride home from the federal courthouse. Sure enough, Hand swore a blue streak.

One day Ruth spoke up. "Judge Hand, in this car you speak

freely—you say words my mother never taught me. I don't seem to be inhibiting you."

The lesson was lost on Hand, who replied, "Young lady, I'm not *looking* at you."

A SWEDISH DETOUR

By this time, more doors at corporate law firms were opening to women, but Ruth's horizons were expanding and she was no longer interested in working at one.

Thanks, but no thanks.

She *was* ready for a challenge, though. In 1961 a Dutch man she knew from Columbia Law School, Hans Smit, invited her to lunch at the Harvard Club (where women had to enter by the side door). He was putting together a project at Columbia comparing the American legal systems with those in France, Italy, and Sweden.

Smit made her an unusual offer: "Ruth, how would you like to coauthor a book about civil procedure in Sweden?" It turned out that while he had no trouble lining up men to go to France and Italy, he couldn't find anyone willing to become fluent in Swedish and journey there to study the legal system.

Intriguing! Ruth knew little about Sweden, much less its language, but she was game. Writing a book was a lifelong goal, and here was the opportunity. Also, she had never really lived on her own. Could she manage? Jane was entering first grade, a little more independent now. Marty agreed to hold down the fort at home and promised that he and Jane would come and visit her in Sweden.

A NEW WORLD FOR WOMEN?

A Swedish city judge met her at the airport in Stockholm, and Ruth's adventure began. When she looked around her, she saw women living different lives from what she knew back home. After World War II, women in Sweden had taken jobs in larger numbers than American women had. And Swedish working women were questioning the restrictions against them.

As a Swedish journalist named Eva Moberg pointed out, women in Sweden now had two jobs, while men still had the one. It wasn't fair: "Actually, there is no biological connection whatsoever between the function of giving birth to and nursing a child and the function of washing its clothes, preparing its food, and trying to bring it up to be a good and harmonious person," wrote the journalist. "Both men and women have one main role: that of being human beings."

Ruth began to sense that another world was possible for women, a world where they could strike back against unfair conditions, where activists could push the government to free men and women from rigid gender roles.

She learned something about herself too in her first six weeks in Sweden. She could do just fine on her own.

Back in New York, Smit encouraged Ruth to overcome her shyness by speaking at international conferences and lecturing at some civil procedure classes at Columbia. She went on to coauthor and publish what was called the best English-language book on the Swedish judicial system. (Okay, it was the only such book at that time. But still.)

Maybe Ruth didn't realize it then, but her work in Sweden wasn't a detour at all. It changed her life. It transformed how she thought about women, men, and the world—though it would be a while before she did anything about it.

ANOTHER DETOUR, TO NEW JERSEY

Columbia Law School, where Ruth was lecturing, had no women professors. But in 1963, a professor there gave her a heads-up: Rutgers University Law School in Newark, New Jersey, was looking to add a woman professor. Only fourteen women in the entire country had permanent positions at law schools—and one was already at Rutgers.

RUTH B. GINSBURG
Assistant Professor of Law
B.A. Cornell Univ.
LL.B. Columbia Univ.

Ruth got the job. Soon after, she and her fellow professor Eva Hanks were profiled in the *Newark Star-Ledger* under the headline "Robes for Two Ladies." The story started by calling them "slim, attractive" and went on to observe, "from their youthful appearance, they could easily be taken for students." It didn't say much about their actual work.

Sexism still ruled. In her first year, Rutgers offered Ruth an annual contract to teach civil procedure.

"They told me 'We can't pay you as much as A., [a man] who

has three children; you have a husband who earns a good salary,'" said Ruth later. According to the university, "It was only fair to pay me modestly, because my husband had a very good job."

She tried to object: "I asked if B., a bachelor, was also paid more, and was told, 'yes.'" End of conversation. She was getting short-changed, but there wasn't much she could do for now.

Ruth plunged into work, every day boarding the train from Manhattan to Newark. Her commute was an excellent place, it turned out, to churn through paperwork. She published articles with thorny titles like "Recognition and Execution of Foreign Civil Judgments and Arbitration Awards."

She got renewed for a second year.

WEARING BAGGY CLOTHES

Then, in 1965, she discovered she was pregnant again. Ruth and Marty were caught by surprise—after his cancer treatment they hadn't been sure they could have more children. They had just about convinced ten-year-old Jane that being an only child wasn't really such a bad deal.

Ruth was thrilled, but also nervous about her job. Would Rutgers renew her contract if they knew she was pregnant? She'd hate to make the same mistake she'd made in Oklahoma—revealing her pregnancy too soon. So she started to wear baggy clothes from her mother-in-law, who was a size larger.

Luckily, no one seemed to notice. She waited until the last day of classes, with the next year's contract in her hand, to break the news to her colleagues.

James was born on September 8, and Ruth was soon back teaching her classes.

LEARNING FRoM HER OWN STUDENTS

Ruth was noticing changes in the students she taught. When she had first started at Rutgers there were maybe five or six women in her classes. But with men being drafted or volunteering for the Vietnam War, more and more women were filling up the law school seats.

At Rutgers School of Law, where RBG began teaching in 1963

Certain books were firing the students up—like Simone de Beauvoir's *The Second Sex* and Betty Friedan's *The Feminine Mystique.* Ruth had read them too. They questioned and rebelled against the narrow roles set out for women, including being denied a career.

Many of the students had gone south to work alongside African Americans denied the right to vote by a racist system. But both white and black women came to see that even among their brothers in the movement, old attitudes about a woman's place ruled. (Of course, women of color had to bear a double burden.)

The world was slowly, creakily starting to change. The Civil Rights Act of 1964 at long last made it illegal for employers to discriminate against people because of the color of their skin. Keeping people out of jobs because of their gender was also made illegal in the same law, but congressmen tended to treat that part as a subject for jokes.

Then, in 1968, the administration of President Lyndon B. Johnson added discrimination on the basis of gender to the list of offenses that would endanger federal funding, and people started to take it more seriously.

Always a quick study, Ruth was learning from her own students. What she had accepted, they refused to put up with. When a group of young female law students came to her in 1970 and asked her to teach the first-ever Rutgers class on women and the law, she was quick to agree.

As always, the first thing Ruth did was head to the library. She wanted to research what had been published in this area so far. It took her only a month to read every federal court decision and every article about the way the law viewed women. There wasn't much to read, and what was there wasn't very helpful. One popular textbook, while straining for an analogy, included the sentence "Land, like woman, was meant to be possessed."

Clearly, the new class she was going to teach on women and the law was much needed!

A MAJOR COUP

Ruth, perhaps motivated by her students, was herself ready for a rebellion: she was through being underpaid by Rutgers just because she was a woman. She helped the other female professors file a federal class-action pay-discrimination claim against the university. That meant that a group of women banded together to make the case that it was a problem bigger than just one of them.

And they won. Professors, no matter if they were male or female, would get equal pay for equal work. The university even paid them what they should have made in the first place, known as back pay.

Putting in nine years at Rutgers, Ruth was making a name for herself.

In 1972, over in New York City, Columbia Law School finally saw the light. It hired her as its first tenured female professor—a job for life. According to the *New York Times*, Columbia had "scored a major coup: its law school, to its undisguised glee, has just bid for and won a woman for the job of full professor." After all, according to the dean of the law school, "Mrs. Ginsburg" was actually qualified, apparently unlike all the other women they had refused to hire in 114 years of existence.

Some of her new colleagues turned up their noses, quick to label Ruth as a case of affirmative action—a program intended to fix historical injustice, which they saw as letting in less-qualified people.

"There was a certain hostility to having her there," said one student, "and the notion that she was only there because of the pressure the school faced to hire a woman."

Ruth was well aware that some people considered affirmative action to be a bad thing. "Others were of the view," she later wrote a bit delightedly, "that at last, the days of 'negative action' were over."

RUTH GETS BUSY AT COLUMBIA

The women at Columbia, on the other hand, had been waiting for her and began contacting her for help. Women employees at Columbia got lower pay and lower pension benefits than men. There was no such thing as pregnancy coverage in their health insurance plans.

Ruth was on the case—literally. She helped file *another* class-action lawsuit with one hundred named plaintiffs on behalf of female teachers and administrators at the university.

She prevailed, and they won.

In another case, the university was about to lay off more than two dozen maids, mostly women of color—but not a single male janitor. Ruth wrote to Columbia's president, calling the firing of the maids "a grave and costly mistake." She urged him to "avoid a course destined to turn into a federal case"—namely a lawsuit.

Besides showing up at meetings to advocate for the maids, Ruth got the New York branch of the American Civil Liberties Union involved. The ACLU is a nonprofit national organization that takes legal action "to defend and preserve the individual rights and liberties guaranteed to every person in this country by the Constitution and laws of the United States." Ruth had signed up with the ACLU as volunteer lawyer a few years earlier.

The Columbia professor who had helped Ruth to get her job at Rutgers was furious. In a letter to the "gentlemen" of the ACLU, he accused the group of rushing—"to begin screaming prematurely"—to accuse the university of sex discrimination.

Ruth was furious too. In the margins of the professor's letter she scribbled, "He misconceives nature of the case. No!!!"

That's right, three exclamation points. Do not mess with Ruth.

She took on the fight, and in the end none of the maids were fired.

RBG's Exercise Routine,
Part 1

Beginning at age twenty-nine, Ruth has made a concerted effort to keep her body as strong as her mind. She took up the popular Royal Canadian Air Force exercise plan, performing it daily ever after. It required quick spurts of:

- ★ toe touching

- ★ knee raising

- ★ arm circling

- ★ leg lifting

- ★ and more—stretching, sit-ups, push-ups, back extensions, and running in place

5

Women Are People, Too

A certain office in New Jersey was being deluged with letters from frustrated women:

★   *a Lipton Tea worker barred from adding her family to her insurance plan because the company assumed only married men had people who depended on them*

★   *girls who weren't allowed to enter Princeton University's summer engineering program*

★   *the best tennis player in Teaneck, who was not allowed on the varsity team because she was a girl*

★ *teachers forced out of their jobs the moment they started showing their pregnancies, and sometimes before, then sometimes getting their jobs back and sometimes not, at the schools' whim*

★ *a military woman who received an honorable discharge for being pregnant, but when reenlisting after giving birth was told that pregnancy was "a moral and administrative disqualification"*

★ *a female letter carrier forced to wear a beret or pillbox hat, not the male carrier hat that actually kept the sun out of her eyes*

These weren't new dilemmas—what was new was that women were finally speaking up. No one had thought complaining about it would make any difference. Ruth wanted to help, and she knew she was in a very good position to do so.

Ruth Bader Ginsburg was on it, solving cases in the 1970s, like a certain girl detective.

NANCY DREW RIDES AGAIN

The office getting all the letters was the New Jersey branch of the American Civil Liberties Union.

Ruth was still teaching, shaping young minds in her stellar academic career. But she made an agreement with the university that she be allowed to work with the ACLU helping people—especially women enduring discrimination—with their court cases.

Her work had a sharp new focus, and the ACLU gave her a platform to use it.

Ruth and her colleagues began sending strongly worded letters to advocate for the women who were being discriminated against. But such letters soon came to seem futile to her, like trying to catch the ocean in a thimble. There would always be another sexist law or regulation to take down. She and the other advocates for women's rights needed to think bigger.

Was it possible that the Constitution had the solution? This document, along with its twenty-seven amendments, spelled out how the United States was to be governed. The Constitution began with "We the people." And women *were* people, even if they had been long prevented from living out their full destinies.

RBG at Rutgers

Ruth had her eye on the Fourteenth Amendment to the Constitution, which in 1868 defined citizenship and guaranteed equal protection to all males, at least on paper. It had never been applied to mean *women* had equal rights, but that didn't mean Ruth wasn't going to try.

RUTH AND MARTY TEAM UP

One night, when Jane and James were in bed, Ruth was working in the bedroom as usual when Marty called from the dining room, where he was working: "There's something you've got to read!" By this time, he was a prominent New York tax lawyer.

"I don't read tax cases," she replied, but reluctantly she agreed.

RBG at the ACLU of New Jersey

Charles Moritz was a traveling book salesman who lived with his elderly mother in Denver. When he was on the road he paid someone to care for her, but when he tried to take the payment as a tax deduction, the Internal Revenue Service (IRS) said no way. Moritz was a bachelor, and the IRS granted such deductions only to women, widowers, or married men.

The notion that a man on his own might be responsible for taking care of his family? It seemed ridiculous to many at the time.

Ruth grinned and said, "Let's take the case." It was to be the only time she and Marty worked together as lawyers.

It might have seemed odd that this champion of women would take a man's case. But the case was right up Ruth's alley. The government said that Charles Moritz had to pay more just because he was a man. If a court agreed and said this was wrong, it would set a precedent Ruth could use in future cases.

Ruth wrote to Mel Wulf, an old friend from summer camp (he still called her Kiki), who had become the national legal director of the ACLU. He agreed to use ACLU resources to back the Ginsburgs. Later Wulf would brag that he had "plucked Ruth Ginsburg from obscurity."

Briefs are the written docu-ments presented to a court that argue why one party in the case should win. In their brief taking the case to court, the Ginsburgs argued that the government couldn't discriminate between men and women "when biological differences are not related to the activities in question." The Ginsburgs won the case at the Court of Appeals level, the last stop for cases that don't go all the way to the Supreme Court.

The sexist law was changed.

RBG at work

DROPPING A HINT

When Ruth sent the brief to Wulf, she wrote, "Some of this should be useful for *Reed v. Reed*"—an upcoming case close to her heart. Ruth cleverly added a hint to her note: "Have you thought about whether

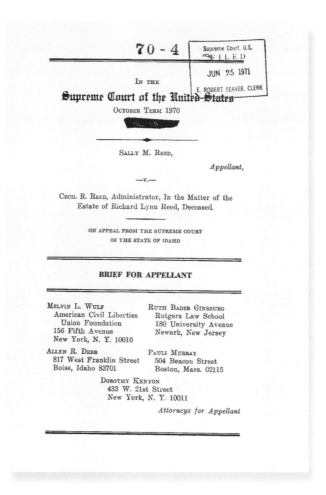

70 - 4

Supreme Court, U.S.
FILED

JUN 25 1971

E. ROBERT SEAVER, CLERK

IN THE

Supreme Court of the United States

OCTOBER TERM 1970

SALLY M. REED,

Appellant,

—v.—

CECIL R. REED, Administrator, In the Matter of the
Estate of Richard Lynn Reed, Deceased.

ON APPEAL FROM THE SUPREME COURT
OF THE STATE OF IDAHO

BRIEF FOR APPELLANT

MELVIN L. WULF	RUTH BADER GINSBURG
American Civil Liberties	Rutgers Law School
Union Foundation	180 University Avenue
156 Fifth Avenue	Newark, New Jersey
New York, N. Y. 10010	
ALLEN R. DERR	PAULI MURRAY
817 West Franklin Street	504 Beacon Street
Boise, Idaho 83701	Boston, Mass. 02115

DOROTHY KENYON
433 W. 21st Street
New York, N. Y. 10011

Attorneys for Appellant

it would be appropriate to have a woman co-counsel in that case???"

In other words, could she write the brief for this important case—a high-stakes one on its way to the Supreme Court? She had never reached so high.

It was rare for Ruth to ask anyone to consider her because of her gender.

But to get to the Supreme Court? Definitely worth it.

It was *Reed v. Reed* that was going to put her on the map.

Years later, Wulf had to admit, "Maybe I didn't pluck her from obscurity. Maybe she plucked herself from obscurity."

STANDING ON SHOULDERS

Someone else shaping Ruth's thinking at the time was Pauli Murray, whom she had met during her summer at a law firm. As a black civil rights attorney, Murray was trying to build a bridge between the civil rights movement—which she saw as being dominated by sexist men—and women's rights activists, many of whom she saw as having serious blind spots on race.

As early as 1961 Murray had been arguing that the Fourteenth Amendment, granting equal protection under the law, could very well be the key to freeing women of legal constraints. She was an inspiration to Ruth, who taught Murray's articles in her classes.

Civil rights activist Pauli Murray, who inspired RBG

In 1966, Murray and another ACLU attorney, Dorothy Kenyon, challenged the all-white and all-male jury in Alabama that had acquitted the murderers of two civil rights activists. Even after slavery had been abolished, the whites in power made sure they would keep it by blocking black people from voting and serving on juries.

At the time, jury duty was optional for women, because they were "still regarded as the center of home and family life," according to the courts. The Supreme Court had never said it was unconstitutional to discriminate against women, on the view that their bodies justified different treatment. The law hadn't made much progress in this area since 1948, when Ruth's old nemesis Felix Frankfurter had written an opinion holding that allowing women to become bartenders could "give rise to moral and social problems."

Murray and Kenyon won their case. The appeals court ruled that Alabama had to allow African American men and women to serve on juries. But Alabama never took the case on to the Supreme Court—so the story ended there, a victory without setting further precedent.

Now Ruth wanted to build on their work in her *Reed v. Reed* brief.

THE PLIGHT OF SALLY REED

Sally Reed, a woman living in Boise, Idaho, had a son who committed suicide in his teens. When the boy died, his father, Cecil Reed, oversaw his estate—because he was a man.

Ruth was fighting for Sally Reed. As she wrote the brief for another lawyer to present at the Supreme Court, Ruth crafted her best arguments. Her writing was sprinkled with references not usually found at the Supreme Court—the French feminist writer Simone de Beauvoir; the British poet Alfred, Lord Tennyson; the Swedish sociologist Gunnar Myrdal; and the antislavery and women's rights activist Sojourner Truth.

She also took the unusual step of putting Pauli Murray's and Dorothy Kenyon's names on the cover as coauthors. She wanted to make it clear that she was "standing on their shoulders," as she put it.

"It's just not done," an ACLU colleague scolded her.

"I don't care," she replied. "They deserve recognition." In arguing for the law to view men and women equally, she was carrying on the work of these pioneers.

But was the world finally ready to listen?

One November night in 1971, an exhausted Ruth was coming home on the train from a day of teaching. She looked up briefly from her work and noticed the headline on the front page of a nearby man's newspaper: "High Court Outlaws Sex Discrimination."

She had won!

This was a landmark victory in Supreme Court history—the first time it had ever struck down a law that treated men and women unequally. A very big deal.

At the ACLU's Women's Rights Project

WOMEN WORKING

Unfortunately, the court's ruling was narrow—it had set forth no broader rule that would cover other cases, leaving the law ambiguous. Ruth still had more work to do. Plenty more cases were awaiting, and a huge one was about to drop in her lap.

After her *Reed* victory, Ruth helped found the ACLU Women's Rights Project, becoming its codirector. The WRP would take on the ambitious mission of fighting for women's equality, with a focus on public education, the law, and bringing cases to court—even to the Supreme Court if necessary—with the help of local ACLU groups across the country.

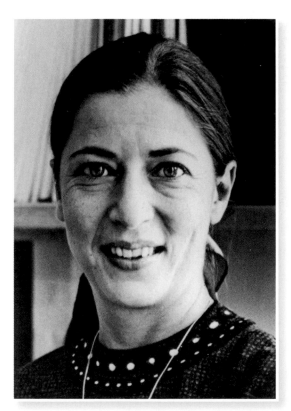

At Columbia in 1972

By this time, the country did have new laws banning discrimination in pay, employment, and education. But Ruth knew that promises on paper wouldn't be enough: "The distance to equal opportunity for women—in the face of the pervasive social, cultural, and legal roots of sex-based discrimination—remains considerable," she wrote in 1972.

Ruth split her time between teaching at Columbia and her new pet project. She plunged into writing the briefs for one case after another. Sometimes she wrote the briefs for other lawyers to argue and sometimes she argued the cases in court herself. All of it was important work that could lead to real change.

Presiding over the WRP's offices on Fortieth Street in New York, her desk was an oasis of calm. The bright yellow sign at the door read "Women Working." Moms were welcome to bring their newborns to the office, to be tended by paid college interns. Ruth loved it all. She was a long, long way from getting pushed out of her job in Oklahoma and scrambling for baggy clothes to keep her job at Rutgers.

The WRP lawyers decided among themselves which of them would appear before the court to make their case. In 1973, Ruth argued a major case in front of the Supreme Court by herself for the first time.

THE BIG TIME

She was so nervous the day of her appearance that she skipped lunch for fear she couldn't keep it down.

Her admissions card to the court that day read "Mrs. Ruth Ginsburg." Ruth had been going by Ms. since the marriage-neutral term Ms. had been invented. Her students who accompanied her that day protested and wanted her to demand a new card. Ruth said no—she was there to win, and she had to pick her battles.

Like a soldier suiting up for war, she wore her mom's circle pin and earrings. How proud Celia would have been to see Ruth that day—a lone woman in front of stone-faced men, asking them to do something they had so far refused to do: recognize that the Constitu-

tion banned sex discrimination.

All arguments at SCOTUS begin the same way: "Mr. Chief Justice, and may it please the court." Ruth was still queasy, and her voice was shaky at first.

Anticipating her case of nerves, she had memorized her opening sentence. She spoke about Sharron Frontiero, an air force lieutenant whose husband, Joseph, had been denied the same housing, medical, and dental benefits as other military spouses. The reason? Sharron was a woman and Joseph was a man.

She took a deep breath and told the justices that with *Frontiero v. Richardson* they had to finish the job they'd started in *Reed v. Reed*. In both of these cases the same stereotype was in play: "The man is or should be the independent partner in a marital unit. The woman, with an occasional exception, is dependent, sheltered from bread-winning experience."

RUTH ON A ROLL

As Ruth went on, she forgot all about her empty stomach, and she felt the ground steadying under her. The nine Supreme Court justices, imposing as they might be, were her captive audience for the next ten minutes. She knew so much more about the case and the topic than they did, she reminded herself, and it was her job to teach them. That was something Ruth knew how to do with confidence. She'd been teaching law for almost a decade.

These distinguished men of the court thought of themselves as good fathers and good husbands. Men and women were fundamen-

tally different, they believed, and women were lucky to be spared the pressures of the real world. Now Ruth, not yet forty, had to make these elderly justices see that women deserved the same standing in the world as men.

On the other side, in its brief, the government defended its policy of assuming women were dependents. After all, most breadwinners were men. The name on the first page of that brief was Erwin Griswold. He was the Harvard Law dean who'd invited Ruth to that humiliating dinner, and now he was the United States Solicitor General.

Ruth had once told Dean Griswold she had gone to law school to better make wifely chitchat with Marty. Now Marty was in the back of the room, silently cheering her on.

Treating men and women differently under the law, she told the justices, implied "a judgment of inferiority." It told women their work was less valuable. "These distinctions have a common effect," she said firmly. "They help keep woman in her place, a place inferior to that occupied by men in our society."

Ruth was on a roll, rattling off case names from previous lawsuits to argue her point.

A MYSTERIOUS SILENCE

This entire time, the judges hadn't said a word. Normally they pepper lawyers with questions, barely allowing them to get a full sentence out.

So Ruth kept on arguing: "Sex, like race, is a visible, immutable characteristic bearing no necessary relationship to ability." These were powerful words, since recent court cases had held that laws that treated people differently on the basis of race were almost always unconstitutional. Were laws that classified what men and women could do blatantly unconstitutional, the same way as laws that classified people by race?

Ruth boldly urged the court to say yes.

Lawyers are given strict time limits to make their cases, and her time was almost up. She looked each of the justices in the eye and quoted Sarah Grimké, the abolitionist and advocate for women's right to vote. "She said, 'I ask no favor for my sex. All I ask of our brethren is that they take their feet off our necks.'"

RBG split her time between Columbia and the ACLU.

Ruth had spoken for ten minutes without a single interruption from the justices. Apparently, she had stunned them into silence.

Were they even listening?

She maintained her composure, but inside she was trembling. As the crowd filed out of the court, Dean Griswold himself approached Ruth and solemnly shook her hand.

That night, one of the justices, who was in the habit of grading the lawyers on their performance, gave Ruth only a C+. "Very precise female," he noted grudgingly.

A BATTLE WON

After her big day at court, Ruth waited some four months for the decision. Justices have a lot on their plates—sorting through thousands of cases to decide which ones they're going to accept, then hearing arguments, researching, and conferring on those cases.

On May 14, 1973, she learned she had won.

The court struck down the rule that treated Sharron Frontiero's work as less important to her family than a male service member's. They might not have showed it in the courtroom, but eight out of the nine justices agreed with Ruth.

Justice William Brennan wrote: "Traditionally, such discrimination was rationalized by an attitude of 'romantic paternalism' which, in practical effect, put women not on a pedestal, but in a cage"—words Ruth herself might have spoken.

In other words, the court rejected the idea that it was okay to treat men and women differently as long as it was framed as a favor, not a restriction.

The lone voice of disagreement, or dissent, was Justice William Rehnquist, who had trouble taking the matter seriously: "My wife became resigned long ago to the idea that she married a male chauvinist pig, and my daughters never pay attention to anything I do."

A male chauvinist pig is a man who doesn't mind showing he believes women are inferior. It was becoming a label most men didn't broadcast, but this justice seemed proud of it.

The same justice later would lamely try to joke with Ruth when she argued another case: "You won't settle for putting Susan B. Anthony on the new dollar?" Only afterward did Ruth come up with the answer she wished she'd shot back at him: "Tokens won't do."

ONE STEP AT A TIME

Frontiero v. Richardson was a stunning victory for Ruth, but she had learned a few things from it. She thought of arguing her cases as trying to teach the justices, and she wouldn't stop doing that. But as she contemplated the road ahead, she acknowledged that "one doesn't learn that lesson in a day. Generally, change in our society is incremental, I think. Real change, enduring change, happens one step at a time."

She would have to cultivate being patient. And maybe being a little deaf, as her mother-in-law had suggested—by ignoring ignorant remarks, even when they came from a justice on the Supreme Court.

Not everyone agreed with Ruth's methods. Her fellow ACLU lawyers were on fire to transform the world, and sometimes they had to be persuaded to see things her way. "She insisted that we attempt

RBG was the first tenured woman at Columbia Law School.

to develop the law one step at a time," Kathleen Peratis said later. "'Present the court with the next logical step,' she urged us, and then the next and the next. 'Don't ask them to go too far too fast, or you'll lose what you might have won.' She often said, 'It's not time for that case.'

"We usually followed her advice, and when we didn't, we invariably lost."

STAYING IN FIGHTING SHAPE

While basically maintaining two careers, Ruth tried to relax whenever she could.

Besides her Royal Canadian Air Force workouts, she went golfing on the weekends with Marty and relished even more strenuous activities, like riding horses. They shared a box at the Metropolitan Opera

House and went about once a month on Friday evenings.

But her work ethic, always stellar, never dimmed. When they went to the movies, she brought a penlight along to read mail during the previews. When golfing, she kept briefs in the golf cart to read between strokes. James would wake in the middle of the night to see his mom scribbling away at legal pads, nibbling on prunes, her favorite snack.

On vacation in the Virgin Islands in 1980

RBG Speaks

"I think that men and women,
shoulder to shoulder,
will work together to make
this a better world. Just as I don't
think men are the superior sex,
neither do I think women are.
I think it is great that we are
beginning to use the talents of all of
the people, in all walks of life,
and that we no longer have the
closed doors that we once had."

6

"Did You Always Want to Be a Judge?"

Ruth learned the same lessons from her clients as she had in her own life: in the law, anything that looked like a favor to women could be used against them. Take pregnancy, which society said was a special gift to women. But if pregnant women needed to support their families or wanted to keep their jobs, the way they were treated didn't feel like such a prize. Ruth's experiences in Oklahoma and at Rutgers had taught her that lesson too well.

With her work on the Women's Rights Project, Ruth went on to fight numerous pregnancy-related cases—arguing for women who were fired or refused promotions for being pregnant and arguing against companies that excluded pregnancy coverage from their

RBG in 1977

health insurance plans. Ruth believed that treating pregnancy as special, even if it was supposed to make it easier for women, would backfire. Instead, she sought broad policies that she hoped would make it harder for employers to single women out for discrimination.

In 1978, Ruth teamed up with her feminist law friends to help pass a groundbreaking law that helped millions of women. The Pregnancy Discrimination Act said that employers had to treat pregnant workers like anyone else who needed to take time off, like for a broken leg.

MOMMY LAUGHED

It was one thing to preach equality. It was another to live it at home.

With the birth of James, Ruth and Marty tried as hard as they could to be home for dinner at seven with the children every night.

They took them to classical music concerts at the New York Philharmonic and other cultural outings around the city.

But while Marty worked his way up the ladder at his law firm, Ruth was the one who walked them to the park and went over their homework every night. However, Ruth told the children's schools, "This child has two parents," and asked them to alternate calls with her husband—which, back then, when dads weren't involved as much as they are now, was unusual.

So it was Marty that the elementary school called when James took the hand-operated elevator for a forbidden ride. Marty was told: "Your son stole the elevator!" "How far could he take it?" was Marty's response.

As a parent, Ruth could be what Jane called "austere." When Jane got in trouble, Ruth's response was to be "real quiet" to indicate her disappointment, much as her own mom had done when Ruth brought home a less-than-perfect report card.

The kids enjoyed trying to make their "austere" mom laugh, and teenage Jane even kept track of the moments in a book called *Mommy Laughed*. Jane once rebelliously announced that she wanted to be a stay-at-home mom like her grandmother. (She later changed her mind.) With great pity, the mother of one of Jane's classmates told her to be extra nice to Jane because "Jane's mommy works." But in fact Ruth's kids were very proud of her. In her high school yearbook, nearly a decade before Ruth was even a judge, Jane listed her ambition as "to see her mother appointed to the Supreme Court. If necessary, Jane will appoint her."

A NEAR CAR CRASH

Ruth's favorite case while with the Women's Rights Project involved a man named Stephen Wiesenfeld. It was one of six cases that Ruth argued herself before the Supreme Court, and three of those cases were about widowers, as it happened.

Stephen Wiesenfeld was a single father whose wife had died in childbirth. Stephen held down the fort at home. His wife, Paula, had supported the family with her work as a teacher. Now Stephen was being denied the government Social Security benefits that would have ordinarily gone to a widow, even though as a widower he was now the sole caretaker of his baby boy, Jason Paul.

Monday, November 27, 1972

The baby, Ruth wrote, was a victim of a law that "includes children with dead fathers, but excludes children with dead mothers." She hadn't forgotten what it felt like to lose her own mother.

She could also

Social Security inequality

To the editor:

Your article about widowed men last week prompted me to point out a serious inequality in the Social Security regulations.

It has been my misfortune to discover that a male can not collect Social Security benefits as a woman can.

My wife and I assumed reverse roles. She taught for seven years, the last two at Edison High School. She paid maximum dollars into Social Security. Meanwhile, I, for the most part, played homemaker.

Last June she passed away while giving birth to our only child. My son can collect benefits but I, because I am not a WOMAN homemaker, can not receive benefits.

Had I been paying into Social Security and, had I died, she would have been able to receive benefits, but male homemakers can not. I wonder if Glora Steinem knows about this?

STEPHEN WIESENFELD,
Edison

relate to Stephen especially well because her marriage was in some ways similar to his. In fact, when Stephen later testified on Justice Ginsburg's behalf in front of Congress, he said that he and his wife, like the Ginsburgs, had been "among the pioneers of alternative family lifestyles"—by which he meant families that defied stereotypes and shared jobs inside and outside the home.

At the Greenbrier resort circa 1972

Months after making the case for Stephen, Ruth was flipping around the dial on her car radio one day on her way to work when she found out that she had won. The Social Security law that treated male and female caregivers differently was unconstitutional. "My first reaction was that I have to get hold of myself or I'll have an accident," she told a reporter that day. "When I got to Columbia, I went running through the halls kissing the students who had worked with me on the case. And I am normally a very unemotional person."

But now, she told a friend, the victory made her cry. She had won justice for Stephen, but she had also gotten one step closer to justice for all.

WALKING THE SUPREME COURT IN HER DIRECTION

This time all the justices were on her side: "The gender-based distinction of this law is entirely irrational," wrote one. Even often-skeptical Justice Rehnquist agreed—although he said he was voting to strike down the law because it harmed the baby.

A triumphant Ruth saw the case as "part of an evolution toward a policy of neutrality—a policy that will accommodate traditional patterns, but at the same time, one that requires removal of artificial constraints so that men and women willing to explore their full potential as humans may create new traditions by their actions."

On April 14, 1975 the decision in Weinberger v. Wiesenfeld will become final. We hope you will join us in a toast to that happy event on

Sunday, April 20
from 4:00 - 7:00
at 150 East 69 St. Apt. 2-G
N.Y., N.Y. 10021

R.S.V.P. to Ruth Bader Ginsburg
280-2036

New traditions like the ones she and Marty had created at home, sharing their lives and goals on an equal footing.

The Women's Rights Project took on hundreds of discrimination cases. With the cases Ruth argued herself or offered supporting arguments for, she said she was helping the law catch up with changes that were already taking place in society. Slowly but surely, she had built a set of precedents—one case building on another—that had walked the justices in her direction, toward recognizing women as people.

Still, plenty of colleagues disapproved of Ruth taking on cases with male plaintiffs. After all, it was the Women's Rights Project, not the men's rights project.

It took a while for people to recognize her genius plan. First, she got the attention of the men on the court with something unexpected: a man saying he had been discriminated against. Then she showed them a radical fact: just as women were held back by gender stereotypes, so were men, and one could not be fully free without the other.

Win-win.

Years later, she was at a dinner party where a guest mentioned that Ruth had worked on behalf of "women's liberation." Ruth turned on him with unusual fierceness: "It is not women's liberation; it is women's and men's liberation."

RBG Speaks

"I am fearful, or suspicious,
of generalizations about the way
women or men are. . . .
They cannot guide me reliably
in making decisions about
particular individuals."

MAKING THE ROAD SMOOTHER FoR oTHERS

Ruth believed that having more women in charge would benefit every-one, including men: "Men need to learn, and they do when women show up in their midst in numbers, not as one-at-a-time curiosities."

She went on to say, "Men need the experience of working with women who demonstrate a wide range of personal-ity characteristics, they need to become working friends with women."

It was 1978, and she was speaking at the twenty-fifth anniversary of women gaining admis-sion to Harvard Law School. In the audience was her very own daugh-ter, Jane, a law student, whose road had been smoother, thanks to her mom. By this time the percentage of women in law schools had risen to thirty percent.

Ruth was in such a good mood that day that she cracked a little joke:

Ms.

September 13

Dear Ruth –

Thank you so much for the book, the idea of going to the conference, your excellent and effective argument — and most of all, just for being there.

You always make me very, very proud. And you change minds.

Best,
Gloria

A note from Ms. *magazine cofounder Gloria Steinem, expressing her gratitude for and fondness of RBG's work*

"I understand some of the men come to Harvard Law School these days because"—she paused—"what better place to find a suitable woman?"

She went on to make a prediction: "All-male retreats are on the wane. I expect, before very long, the old boys will find no escape at judges' conference tables."

Those old boys were about to see her prediction come true.

ON A FAST TRACK

Approaching the 1980s, Ruth was one of the most prominent women's rights lawyers in the country.

At Columbia in 1980

Her career was on a fast track—but to where? The next logical step would be for Ruth to be appointed a judge. Judges have more power than lawyers—they are the ultimate interpreters of the law and the Constitution, deciding which lawyers' arguments prevail. But as many strides as women were making, certain glass ceilings still held. Women could get close enough to see the top, but invisible barriers kept them out, and women judges were few and far between.

Sometime in the 1970s, Ruth had interviewed for a federal district court judge position. Federal district courts are where most court cases, civil and criminal, start, with both sides presenting their evidence in great detail. The judges on these ninety-four courts have to know about all aspects of the law. The screening committee told her she wasn't qualified because she had no experience in financial securities—matters about stocks and bonds.

They seemed unaware that they were dealing with one of the fastest learners on the planet.

Ruth was unfazed. She was actually more interested in the broader legal questions raised by the next court up the ladder, the federal appeals court. This court was where people turn when they want to appeal, or protest, the judgment from a district court. The appeals, or appellate, court determines whether or not the law has been applied correctly in the lower court. Decisions are not made by a jury but by a panel of three judges. There are twelve appeals courts, each serving a region of the country, including the District of Columbia, plus the Federal Circuit, which hears cases from across the country on certain issues. So the cases from the ninety-four district courts funnel into one of the thirteen appeals courts.

The appeals court is the last stop before the Supreme Court. Because SCOTUS takes on so few cases, the appeals court judges just below it are often the final word on the law. District court judges have trials where they have to figure out the *facts*, while appeals court judges can spend more time on ideas and principles. Being a judge on this court sounded like a dream job.

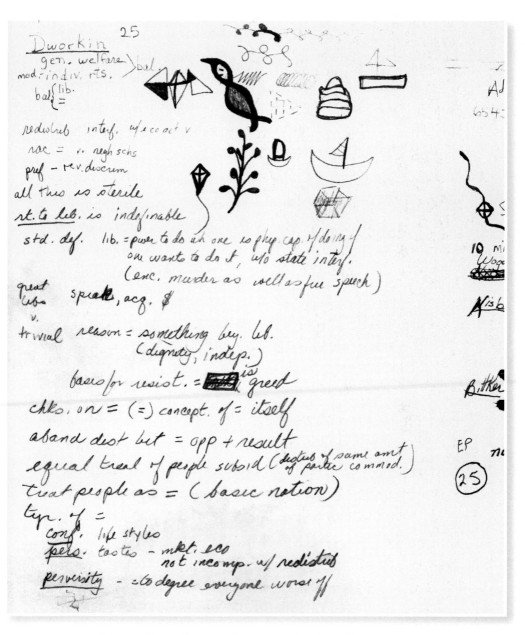

RBG's doodles at the Second Circuit Judicial Conference in 1976

A NEW PRESIDENT

The road to becoming an appeals court judge was a complicated dance—you had to know the right people, which was harder for women when most lawyers, judges, and members of Congress were still men. Then a president has to nominate you, and you have to be confirmed by the United States Senate.

By the time Jimmy Carter became president in 1977, only two women had ever been appointed an appeals court judge: Florence Ellinwood Allen in 1934 and Shirley Mount Hufstedler in 1968. Carter was determined to do better.

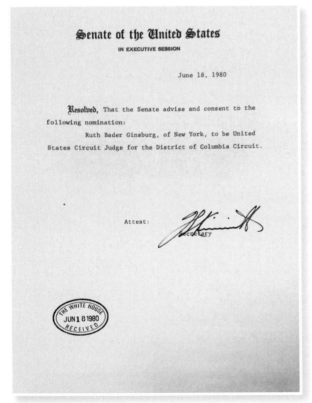

Suddenly, it mattered who Ruth knew— not a guy, but some women in the law. Women who were admirers or former students spoke up in support of Ruth, and some of them were inside the Carter administration, putting in a word for her.

Finally, in 1980, Carter did Ruth the high honor of nominating her as a judge to the United States Court of

Appeals for the District of Columbia Circuit. The D.C. Circuit was sometimes called the most important court in the country after the Supreme Court.

The Senate Judiciary Committee began its debate over Ruth's appointment. One man was afraid that she would have "militant feminist interpretations" of the law, and judges are supposed to be impartial, not take sides in advance. But in the end only one senator in the Judiciary Committee voted against her confirmation, while the full Senate vote was unanimous.

She was in.

"People often ask me, 'Well, did you always want to be a judge?'" said a grateful Ruth. "My answer is that it just wasn't in the realm of the possible until Jimmy Carter became president and was determined to draw on the talent of all of the people, not just some of them."

That was her staid response in public.

In private, the night of her confirmation, she was reveling at a party thrown for her by students and faculty, laughing, sitting on the floor, eating Kentucky Fried Chicken right out of the bucket.

LiFE AS A JuDGE

Another, more serious celebration was held after she was sworn in as a judge. She asked Gerald Gunther, the brilliant Columbia (by then, Stanford) professor who had persuaded a judge to give Ruth her first job, to speak.

Unlike her previous work, this would require her to be objective, judging on the facts of the case, not advocating for particular outcomes.

Ruth, said Gunther, would be "genuinely open-minded and detached" and "heedful of limitations stemming from the judge's own competence."

Some listeners were skeptical. Could Ruth really be a centrist, a moderate, not making her rulings from either a conservative, right point of view or—more likely—a liberal, left point of view?

Gunther, after all these years, was still a gambler. After his talk he bet the skeptics five dollars that in a couple of years, Ruth would "widely be seen as the most independent, thoughtful, modest judge on the bench."

A few years later, he got a five-dollar bill in the mail along

with a newspaper clipping describing Ruth as a solid centrist.

For the next thirteen years, Ruth worked as hard as ever, writing opinions in over three hundred cases.

Her particular appeals court mostly oversaw federal agencies, directly reviewing their decisions and rule making, with cases that were intricate, technical, and—for some of the rest of us—boring. But the issues were important—national security, gun-safety measures, food safety, labor law, election law, and clean-air regulations.

Over the years, people started to forget that she had made her name litigating women's rights. "She was widely regarded not as a 'women's' judge"—as if that was a bad thing—"much less a 'political' judge, but as a judge's judge," wrote two of her clerks.

TOWARD THE MIDDLE

Her reputation as a moderate grew. Sweeping judicial opinions, she believed, could be counterproductive. Popular movements and local legislatures had to be the first to spur social change—otherwise, there would be a backlash against the courts for stepping in.

As always, you couldn't predict Ruth.

In her court, most decisions were made by a panel of three, so they had to be able to reach an agreement. In 1988, a study found that she had voted with the famously conservative Judge Robert Bork in 85 percent of the cases where they been on a panel together. That was compared to the 38 percent of the cases where she voted along with a fellow Carter (more liberal) appointee.

Ruth had to perfect the art of compromise, and she didn't always get every last thing she wanted: "Of course there is a question of bedrock principle where I won't compromise," she said, but she had "learned a lot about other minds [while] paying attention to people's personalities in this job."

Reaching consensus used a different skill set than she had practiced before, and as usual she took it ultraseriously. She even tried to convince her fellow judges that when they all agreed on an opinion, they should leave off the name of the author entirely so the court would appear to speak in a single voice.

No one went for that idea.

"WHY CAN'T YOU BE LIKE MARTY?"

Just as Ruth had moved earlier for the benefit of Marty's work, when he was starting his career as a tax attorney, now Marty took a teaching position in Washington to be with Ruth.

They chose an apartment right across the street from the John F. Kennedy Center, home to the Washington National Opera, so they could regularly attend performances and dress rehearsals. The melodramatic stories sometimes made Ruth weep. Opera, she found, pro-

vided "a most pleasant pause from the court's heavy occupations." She often visited backstage to cheer the singers, and the opera's president said, "We do consider her, informally, part of the family."

They were also regulars at the theater. The director of the Shakespeare Theatre Company said of Ruth, "She has terrific taste and she's very knowledgeable."

The year that Ruth became a judge, 1980, was also the last year she cooked a meal at home. She'd kept up with her perfunctory cooking—Jane wasn't sure she saw a fresh vegetable until she visited France when she was fourteen—but now Marty completely took over with his gourmet creations.

As Jane had told people when she was a small child, "Mommy does the thinking, and Daddy does the cooking."

Ruth dined well. Her special favorite of all his recipes was pork loin braised in milk.

As a federal appeals court judge in 1984

In their Washington home the shelves held more cookbooks, from floor to ceiling in the living room, than tax books. Marty consumed them like they were mystery novels. His luscious recipes, joked a friend, were "the edible version of the Internal Revenue Code."

Another friend said, "I hate Marty Ginsburg." It wasn't out of jealousy of his "lifelong love affair with this wonderful woman." No,

Photograph taken at the Ginsburgs':
© Mariana Cook 1998

"it's because he cooks." In his own house, the friend complained, his wife always asked him, "Why can't you be like Marty?"

Remember how it took Ruth five tries to pass her drivers' test? Well, one day she crashed her car into a gate. After that, Marty begin giving her a lift to the federal courthouse every day.

He read tons of books and told her which ones were worth her time. At parties, where she was still shy, he guided her around the room so they could gracefully mingle.

And he often dragged her out of the office when he felt she needed a break. Once their children were on their own, he'd start calling her at seven thirty—she just had one more thing to take care of—and was usually able to cajole her into coming home for dinner by nine.

When she stayed up too late working, he urged her to get some sleep. "You have to eat one meal a day and you should go to sleep sometimes," he insisted.

MARTY BEHIND THE SCENES

Ruth never took her husband, and the way he boosted her confidence, for granted: "The principal advice that I have gotten from Marty throughout my life is that he always made me feel like I was better than I thought myself. I started out by being very unsure. Could I do this brief? Could I make this oral argument?"

But nowadays, said Ruth, "I look at my colleagues and I say, 'It's a hard job, but I can do it at least as well as those guys.'"

About twelve years after she became a judge, Marty was doing everything in his power—mainly making calls to those he knew at law firms, in Congress and the White House—to make sure that Bill Clinton, the new president of the United States, heard a lot about a certain federal Court of Appeals judge.

After all, it was the president who nominated candidates for the Supreme Court.

How to Be Like RBG

WORK FOR WHAT YOU BELIEVE IN

When RBG sees injustice in the world, she uses her abilities to help change it. The forces of "apathy, selfishness, or anxiety that one is already overextended" are "not easy to surmount," she admits. But we have to try. She urges us "to repair tears in [our] communities, nation, and world, and in the lives of the poor, the forgotten, the people held back because they are members of disadvantaged or mistrusted minorities."

PICK YOUR BATTLES

RBG survived the indignities of prefeminist life mostly by deciding that anger was counterproductive. Besides relying on advice from her mother and mother-in-law, she found a certain First Lady inspirational: "This wonderful woman whose statue I have in my chambers, Eleanor Roosevelt, said, 'Anger, resentment, envy. These are emotions that just sap your energy. They're not productive and don't get you anyplace, so get over it.'" To be like RBG, save your public anger for when there's lots at stake and when you've tried everything else.

DON'T BURN YOUR BRIDGES

"Fight for the things that you care about," RBG advises young people, "but do it in a way that will lead others to join you." She always tells her clerks to paint the other side's argument in the best light, avoiding personal insults. She is painstaking in presenting facts, on the theory that the truth is weapon enough.

DON'T BE AFRAID TO TAKE CHARGE

RBG believes that "women belong in all places where decisions are being made." Back when many feminists were arguing that women had different ways of thinking and expressing themselves because of their biology, she observed the flaw in describing women as inherently different or even purer than men. She was mistreated in her own life and told it was for her own good. So she has used her positions within the establishment to fight for structural change and on behalf of the oppressed.

THINK ABOUT WHAT YOU WANT, THEN DO THE WORK

When young Ruth was suddenly faced with the prospect of starting law school with a toddler, her father-in-law told her, "If you really want to study the law, you will find a way. You will do it." Today RBG says, "I've approached everything since then that way. Do I want this or not? And if I do, I'll do it."

THEN ENJOY WHAT MAKES YOU HAPPY

RBG gets out—a lot.

BRING ALONG YOUR CREW

"RBG was never in it to be the only one, to be the superstar that nobody could match," said a fellow feminist lawyer. RBG mentored legions of feminist lawyers and happily welcomed Sonia Sotomayor and Elena Kagan to the Supreme Court—and would welcome more.

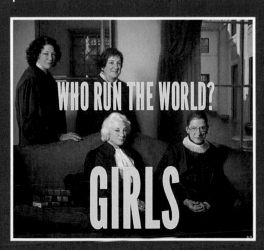

HAVE A SENSE OF HUMOR

Obviously.

7

A Hero, a Star, and a
Supreme Court Justice

The tension was unbearable. It was a Friday in June 1993, and Ruth was looking forward to a break from work—attending a weekend wedding in Vermont. But there was a hitch.

That was the same weekend that President Bill Clinton was expected to finalize his first Supreme Court appointment. Names of several candidates had leaked to the press, though not Ruth's. Still, she had a feeling she was in the running. Should she keep her plans for Vermont or stay in Washington?

Then a White House lawyer called to tell her she could feel free to go: her presence wouldn't be needed in Washington. Clinton had pondered his choice, and he had settled on someone—yet another

man—even though one woman, Sandra Day O'Connor, had joined the court by this time.

It was disappointing, but at least Ruth's dilemma seemed solved. She took off for Vermont.

A WIDE GRIN

Hours later, Ruth got another call from the White House. Could she come back to Washington as soon as possible?

She was assured that her casual outfit (pants) was fine because Clinton would be coming straight off the golf course. Instead, he was dressed in a suit and tie, having just attended a church service. She was mortified. Luckily, it was a true meeting of the minds. "It wasn't just stuff that she had written," he said later, "it was way more than just an intellectual concern of hers. She got the actual human impact of these decisions."

It was nearly midnight when the president tried to call Ruth Bader Ginsburg to tell her he was nominating her to the Supreme Court. (It took three tries, thanks to a connection problem.) "I feel really good about this," he told her. One more thing: The ceremony would be the very next morning. "Just speak from your heart and mind tomorrow," he advised her.

The process of checking into Ruth's background went smoothly—no skeletons in the closet, no financial conflicts of interest. When White House staff came to their apartment to check their tax returns, they gave Marty credit for the Ginsburgs' meticulous records. In fact it was Ruth who handled their personal finances, presenting files for the staffers to rifle through.

Marty did make them all a nice lunch.

In the White House Rose Garden, Clinton introduced Ruth to the American public as a hero to the women's movement and a legal star. Above all, he said, he had chosen her because she was a moderate, someone whose "moral imagination has cooled the fires of her colleagues' discord."

Squinting behind her enormous violet-tinted glasses, dressed as elegantly as ever, Ruth had a grin that was uncharacteristically wide.

"Ruth Bader Ginsburg cannot be called a liberal or a conservative," Clinton went on in his song of praise. "She has proved herself too thoughtful for such labels. Having experienced discrimination, she devoted the next twenty years of her career to fighting it and making this country a better place for our wives, mothers, our sisters, and our daughters."

(Not that she would have interrupted the president, but Ruth might have added here, "And our husbands, our fathers, our brothers, and our sons.")

Ruth took her spot at the podium to offer her heartfelt thanks. She thanked the women's movement "that opened doors for people like me" as well as "the civil rights movement of the 1960s from which the women's movement drew inspiration." She referred to her favorite theme: "The announcement the president just made is significant, I believe, because it contributes to the end of the days when women, at least half the talent pool in our society, appear in high places only as one-at-a-time performers."

She continued speaking from the heart, honoring her biggest influence: "I have a last thank-you. It is to my mother, Celia Amster Bader, the bravest and strongest person I have known, who was taken from me much too soon. I pray that I may be all that she would have been had she lived in an age when women could aspire and achieve and daughters are cherished as much as sons."

Several people in the audience, including Bill Clinton, wiped tears from their eyes.

Ruth had gotten to carry on her mother's memory before the country. She had even helped a man defy gender stereotypes.

FOUR DAYS IN JULY

The public soon weighed in.

One retired justice wrote, "The president could not have made a better choice." Some of the comments were obviously sexist. One journalist called her a "sweet lady," while Harvard Law professor Alan Dershowitz used words like *picky*, *impatient*, and *schoolmarmish*. (As of this writing, no one has come up with a male counterpart to *schoolmarmish*.)

With then-Senator Joe Biden in 1993

For four days in July, Ruth kept her cool throughout her confirmation process. She had to field dozens of vexing questions from the senators about potential court cases. Her answers were precise, delivered with her unusual rhythm: a few words at a time, then a pause while she pinpointed her next ones. Her answers about specific cases were clear: "Time and again, she would say, 'I would apply the law to the facts of the case to the best of my abilities,'" said a clerk who sat in on the hearings. "Coming from some people that might be evasive. Anyone who knew her knows that she means what she said." In fact, her stance set a precedent for future hearings. SCOTUS nominees ever since Ruth have followed what came to be known as the Ginsburg rule: "No hints, no forecasts, no previews," as she put it.

At her confirmation hearings in 1993,
RBG holds up her grandson's work.

Fans were happy to testify on her behalf, like her former client Stephen Wiesenfeld. Some testified against her, like the anti-abortion activist who accused her of a "tendency to be acutely aware of sex discrimination, not for males, but only for females." (Not only false, but absurd: just the opposite criticism from her ACLU days.)

She testified on her own behalf, telling endearing, charming family stories, even boasting about a book made by her grandson called *My Grandma Is Very Special*.

At Senator Edward Kennedy's prompting, Ruth talked about some of the sexist slights she'd experienced over the years. Even now at cocktail parties, the host would introduce someone to Judge Ginsburg and a hand would automatically extend to Marty instead of her. James had gotten used to people asking him what his father did for a living and having to retort that his mom did something interesting, too.

Ruth introduced Marty to the nation with the phrase she always used: her "life's

RBG with her family at her swearing-in in 1993

partner." Supportive as ever, he carried her briefcase into the Senate hearing room every day and spread out her papers on the desk. He wouldn't need to drive her to work anymore. Once she was on the Supreme Court, she would get her own car and driver—one of the perks of the job.

After all the wrangling, when her nomination reached the Senate floor, only three of the one hundred senators voted against her.

DAILY RITUALS of A SECRET CLUB

Ruth took her seat on the Supreme Court on August 10, 1993.

Now she was allowed into the room, the special room where, decades before, nine men had discussed the fate of cases she'd argued.

She was right there where the justices shut the door and say what they really think in conference. Here they vote and decide cases. No one is allowed in this room but the justices themselves—"no secretary, no law clerk, not even a message bearer," said Ruth. Whatever comes out of this confidential meeting comes from one of them. The only records are handwritten notes, if the justices choose to take them.

Ruth loves the rituals and traditions of the court and has revealed a few glimpses.

A buzzer rings five minutes before the justices take their seats at the bench, the closest thing the court comes to facing the public. (And you have to be inside the courtroom to see them in action—absolutely no TV cameras allowed.) They make their way to the Robing Room, paneled in American white oak, to don their heavy black robes. Each justice has a locker that bears his or her name written on a gold plaque.

Ruth likes the standard black robes the judges wear to signal their uniformity: "It's a symbol; we are all in the business of impartial judging." Judges shouldn't wear royal robes of red or maroon, they should wear plain black. She usually orders her robes from England, a particular lord mayor's robe she likes.

Once enrobed, the justices shake hands with one another before lining up in order of seniority and shuffling into the court chamber. To Ruth, this is "a way of saying we are all in this together"—a symbol of the cordial relationship she treasures. So what, as she put it, if another justice responded to you negatively with a "spicy dissenting opinion"? The ideals of the court, of fairness and justice, transcend the daily tempers.

In the courtroom, US marshals with buzz cuts scowl the visitors into silence. At the pound of a gavel at precisely ten a.m., everyone snaps to their feet. A marshal cries, "Oyez, oyez, oyez!"—meaning "hear ye," a medieval call for silence—and then: "All persons having business before the Honorable, the Supreme Court of the United States, are admonished to draw near and give their attention, for the Court is now sitting. God save the United States and this Honorable Court."

The judges take their places, again in order of seniority, in black high-backed chairs on the winged mahogany bench. Below are ceramic spittoons, a holdover from the days when men used to spit a lot in public.

Oral arguments begin. Ruth quickly became known for often asking the first question of the lawyers. It is usually incisive, even if people have to strain to hear her. Said a lawyer who frequently argued before the court: "Her tiny size and quiet voice—combined with the bad acoustics of the courtroom—can mislead visitors . . . into underestimating the justice."

It's not a mistake that smart lawyers make twice.

After the lawyers are done, the justices retire to their chamber to discuss the cases and take a preliminary vote. Once the chief justice has summarized the case, the rest speak their piece in order of seniority. Who is in the majority, and who is in the minority?

Not much debate happens in this room, according to Ruth, despite the hope of outsiders that justices are dueling and debating like mad. "One justice or another will say, after we've talked for several minutes . . . 'It will come out in the writing,'" said Ruth. The chief justice assigns someone to write an opinion, unless he is in the minority, at which point the responsibility falls to the most senior justice in the majority.

A BIG SISTER

For her first twelve years, Sandra Day O'Connor had to scurry back to her chambers when she had to use the bathroom. The bathroom by the Robing Room was men only. With Ruth's arrival the court added a women's bathroom—not just as a practical matter, but as Ruth pointed out, "a sign women were there to stay." Having women on the Supreme Court was not going to be a fluke.

Though Ruth and Sandra had hardly anything in common—especially in their political leanings—they formed an instant bond, with Ruth thinking of Sandra as her "big sister."

RBG and Sandra Day O'Connor in 2001

After years of standing in for all women, O'Connor took "enormous pleasure" in welcoming Ruth. She gave Ruth pep talks, like when Ruth was put off by the complexity of the first opinion the chief justice had assigned her to write. When it was time for Ruth to summarize the opinion from the bench, O'Connor (who had taken the opposite side from her "sister") passed her a note: "This is your first opinion for the court. It is a fine one—I look forward to many more." Remembering the comfort that note gave to her on such a nerve-racking day, Ruth did the same for the next two women to join the court, Sonia Sotomayor and Elena Kagan.

The one thing Ruth and Sandra did share was being part of a generation of women who had to be twice as good as a man just to be given a shot. But on the actual issues they parted ways: a study found that in the decade they served together, O'Connor's votes diverged more from Ruth's than from almost any other justice's.

The Jabot

The standard robe is made for a man, with a place for a shirt and tie to show. That's why Ruth decided to jazz up her robe with lace collars, or jabots—and she has many, many of them.

She keeps at least two dozen on an inside shelf in her closet. Some of her jabots speak their own language, depending on her vote that day. There's the glass-beaded velvet bib necklace from Banana Republic she wore on the day she became the Notorious RBG—"it looks fitting for dissent." Also the majority-opinion jabot, a gift from her clerks, which dangles with gold trim and charms—she doesn't get to wear it nearly as often as she likes.

One of her favorites, a simple crocheted white ring, was bought in a museum in Cape Town, South Africa. Another favorite, bought at the Metropolitan Opera gift shop, is a two-pronged copy of a collar worn by one of her favorite tenors.

This was one RBG trend that didn't catch on. She gave a collar as a gift to Sotomayor, a row of lace ending in two lace blossoms with a flap of plain starched white down the center. Sotomayor wore it at her swearing-in ceremony, but afterward returned to an unadorned robe.

And Kagan just wasn't interested: "I think you just have to do what makes you feel comfortable. In my real life I'm not a frilly, lacy person." Ruth didn't hold it against her.

That was just fine with Ruth: it proved that women had diverse views. It meant that people could look and say, "Here are two women. They don't look alike. They don't always vote alike. But here are two women."

And yet, because they *were* women, they were constantly confused with each other, even though they didn't look or sound similar at all. The National Association of Women Judges anticipated the hassle and presented them with "I'm Sandra" and "I'm Ruth" T-shirts.

Professors and lawyers were always flubbing their names. One day, O'Connor just had to speak up: "She's Justice Ginsburg, I'm Justice O'Connor," she said firmly.

But if either woman was *too* firm, she risked being called out. "Once Justice O'Connor was questioning counsel at oral argument," Ruth recalled. "I thought she was done, so I asked a question, and Sandra said: 'Just a minute, I'm not finished.' So I apologized to her and she said, 'It's OK, Ruth. The guys do it to each other all the time, they step on each other's questions.'" (In fact, a 2015 study showed that each woman justice was interrupted an average of three times more often than each of her male colleagues.)

Sure enough, one newspaper headline the next day read, as paraphrased by Ruth, "Rude Ruth Interrupts Sandra."

LET THE WOMEN IN

Ruth was thrilled to take her place on the SCOTUS bench.

Three years into her tenure, in a case dear to her heart, she had a chance to finish something she had started decades before. In the 1970s, she had represented military servicewomen in an ongoing

campaign to get the government to value their work equally. But women still hadn't secured equality in the military. And the government could still treat men and women differently if they had the right excuses.

United States v. Virginia (1996) was Ruth's first major gender-equality case at SCOTUS. The prestigious Virginia Military Institute received applications from high school girls. It always denied them. VMI claimed that admitting women would undermine its mission, which included training cadets by the "adversative method," which the Institute argued couldn't be used to train women. The federal government had filed a discrimination claim, and VMI had gone so far as to set up a meager program at a sister school—the Virginia Women's Institute for Leadership.

It wasn't enough—for Ruth and many others.

During oral argument, a lawyer for the federal government said, "What we have here is a single-sex institution for men that's designed as a place to teach manly values that only men can learn, to show that men can suffer adversity and succeed." On the other hand, we had "a single-sex institution for women that is openly, expressly, deliberately designed to teach to women womanly values, feminine values." The two institutions were unequal and unfair.

Ruth, of course, agreed—the lawyer was speaking the language she had introduced decades earlier. She added, "If women are to be leaders in life and in the military, then men have got to become accustomed to taking commands from women, and men won't be accustomed to that if women aren't let in."

A WELL-EARNED CELEBRATION

Back in chambers, when the justices took a preliminary vote, it came down to 7–1 in favor of the government: the Virginia Military Institute would be ordered to admit women cadets. Justice Clarence Thomas recused himself because he had a son at VMI, and Antonin Scalia, Ruth's frequent sparring partner, was opposed.

The job of writing the majority opinion was assigned to Ruth. In it she was able to gleefully mention earlier cases she herself had won. Scalia dropped the penultimate draft of his dissent in her lap on a Friday afternoon. He was not yet ready to circulate to the court. But he wanted to give her as much time as he could to answer it. Ruth liked to joke that he'd ruined her weekend. But going over it sharpened her own argument. Looking at a situation from an opposing perspective can do wonders for clarifying one's own thoughts.

On the day Ruth read the opinion from the bench, a half dozen clerks were invited up to chambers to celebrate. No champagne greeted them, just one very delighted justice. "It was the work of the court," said one clerk. "It was a good day in the work of the court."

A landmark victory for Ruth—and the country's women and girls.

This was one of her biggest victories to date: "I regard the VMI case as the culmination of the 1970s endeavor to open doors so that women could aspire and achieve without artificial constraints," she said later. Supreme Court decisions matter beyond the specific case and facts at hand. This one set a precedent that you can't keep women out for no good reason.

Some time later, Ruth got a letter from a 1967 graduate of VMI who said he was glad about the decision—he knew plenty of women who were tough enough to make it through. He even hoped his teenage daughter would consider VMI.

A few months later a bulkier envelope arrived from the same man. Inside was a tiny tin soldier dangling from a pin. The man's mother had just died, leaving behind a pin given to all the mothers of VMI graduates.

He thought his mother would've wanted Ruth to have it.

How to Dress Like RBG (Outside of Court)

★ Keep hair out of your face with a scrunchie. Or, on days when you haven't had time to wash your hair, make a splash with a turban.

★ Carry a copy of the Constitution in your purse.

★ Enjoy fancy footwear—RBG prefers Ferragamos and Stuart Weitzman, plus knee-high leather boots.

★ No need to pierce your ears, but do wear interesting earrings—some of her favorites are her mother's.

★ Definitely no tattoos—she was horrified when her granddaughter got nose and multiple ear piercings, but relieved that at least they weren't permanent.

★ In public wear elegant gloves in black or white lace. She started wearing gloves the year of her bout with colorectal cancer. Justice O'Connor advised her: "You're undergoing chemotherapy. That makes you vulnerable to germs. You are attending receptions and shaking any number of hands. At least wear gloves to protect you." Also oversize sunglasses.

★ Wear regal, loosely fitting jackets of brocade or embroidered silk.

8

Laying Down the Law

A SETBACK

Sandra Day O'Connor, a breast-cancer survivor, counseled Ruth from the onset of her struggle. She recommended scheduling chemo treatments for Fridays so Ruth could recover and be back on the bench on Mondays. She told Ruth to stay active, inviting her to her eight a.m. aerobics class. (Ruth, not being a morning person, declined.)

"Everyone rallied around me," Ruth said gratefully. She saw it as proof of the respectful, cordial environment of the court she so cherished. Even no-nonsense Chief Justice Rehnquist called her into his office and offered to keep her "light" on assignments, giving Ruth her pick of opinions to write. (She didn't take him up on the offer to go easy, but did pick two opinions she wanted.)

With Chief Justice William Rehnquist in 1993

Rehnquist (the justice who had sardonically called himself a "male chauvinist pig") had over the years warmed to Ruth's way of thinking. In a case featuring a man needing unpaid time off to care for his sick wife, he wrote an opinion citing Ruth's earlier litigation before SCOTUS *and* her VMI opinion: "Stereotypes about women's domestic roles are reinforced by parallel stereotypes presuming a lack of domestic responsibilities for men," he wrote. "Because employers continued to regard the family as the woman's domain, they often denied men similar accommodations or discouraged them from taking leave."

The language was so similar to Ruth's that Marty jokingly asked if she had written the opinion. Ruth did have a lot to do with Rehnquist's evolution, but she gave him the credit, thinking it also might have had a lot to do with his new role as a grandfather picking up his granddaughters from school for his single-mom daughter.

Ruth made a rapid recovery from her cancer treatment, and the experience gave her a new outlook: "It is as though a special, zestful spice seasons my work and days," she said. "Everything I do comes with a heightened appreciation that I am able to do it."

BITTER AND SURREAL

In 2000, the case of *Bush v. Gore* threw the fate of the American presidency into the laps of the nine justices. The November election between George W. Bush and Al Gore, two very different candidates, was so close that it ended up hinging on one state: Florida, where the results were in dispute and the Gore campaign had demanded a recount. The whole country was on edge, in limbo.

Lawyers on both sides took the case to court. SCOTUS could have chosen to stay out of the Florida recount and left it to the state courts—that's what Ruth voted to do. Instead, at this point mostly conservative, the court hurried into the fray. With so much at stake, the nine justices wrote six opinions. It was wild and surreal—"described as a circus," said Bush's lawyer, "but that is an insult to the discipline of circuses" (and he was the winner).

On December 12, the court halted Florida's recount, allowing its current count to stand. This had the effect of handing Bush the presidency—dramatic proof that the court's decisions have a huge impact on the country.

Gore supporters were crushed and bitter.

DISSENTING WITH FLAIR

Bush v. Gore wasn't unanimous. In fact, it had four dissents. Ruth's dissent was technical, arguing that the matter should have been left

to the state court to decide.

Her writing sounded calm—"The wisdom of the court's decision to intervene and the wisdom of its ultimate determination await history's judgment"—but reading between the lines, she seemed to be calling the majority highly activist hypocrites.

Ruth didn't like talking about the case. She later insisted that the "December storm over the US Supreme Court" was just a blip: "Whatever the tensions were that day," she said, it was time to come together and show that "all of us really do prize this institution more than our own egos."

In other words, let's move on for the sake of the country and the legitimacy of the court.

SMOKING-HOT PEN

But *Bush v. Gore*, it turned out, was the case that helped Ruth turn into a great dissenter with a smoking-hot pen—spurring her rise to "notorious" status. A Photoshopped image, definitely not approved by Ruth, showed her with two middle fingers pointed upward, captioned "I dissent."

One night, soon after this case with her dissent, she and Marty went to see a Broadway play. As they made their way up the aisle for intermission, Ruth in her trademark scrunchie, the theater boomed with applause as people—presumably Gore supporters—rose to their feet in appreciation of her brave stance.

Ruth couldn't help but beam.

Then Marty, professor of tax law and always the joker, whispered loudly, "I bet you didn't know there was a convention of tax lawyers in town"—playfully assuming the applause was for him.

Just as playfully, Ruth whacked her husband in the stomach.

Marty loved to tell this story, saying that it "fairly captures our

RBG hugs Marty during her ten-year Supreme Court law clerk reunion.

nearly fifty-year happy marriage." It was a story about her, and people admiring her for standing up for what she believed in. But it was also about Marty being irreverent and funny, bringing out a side of her that no one saw unless he was there.

ODD COUPLE

A justice she usually disagreed with fiercely was Antonin Scalia, appointed by Ronald Reagan in 1986, so many people were surprised that he was the one with whom she developed the closest relationship.

Scalia was conservative and acerbic, where Ruth was liberal and mild mannered. He was *so* staunchly conservative that when he entered a room, liberals tended to edge to the opposite side.

But he made Ruth laugh with his witticisms: "I was fascinated by him because he was so intelligent and so amusing. You could resist his position, but you just had to like him." She called him Nino and acknowledged their differences: "I love him, but sometimes I'd like to strangle him."

For his part, Scalia called her "an intelligent woman and a nice woman and a considerate woman—all the qualities that you like in a person."

Since their days serving on the D.C. Circuit Court together, and in spite of their differing constitutional philosophies, "I have always enjoyed Nino," said RBG, using Scalia's nickname. When they were on the road, he was even her shopping buddy. Said Scalia: "If you can't disagree ardently with your colleagues about some issues of law and yet personally still be friends, get another job, for Pete's sake."

They bonded over a shared love of the opera and "our reverence for the Constitution and the institution we serve," said Ruth. The two attended the opera together, even appearing together onstage.

Their unlikely friendship is the subject of its own opera, *Scalia/
Ginsburg.*

Every New Year's Eve, the Scalias and the Ginsburgs, plus their
kids and grandkids, had dinner together. Scalia would bring the

With Scalia onstage at the opera

game from his latest hunting trip, and Marty would whip up a feast.
Said Ruth's grandson: "I never heard them talk about anything political or ideological, because there would be no point."

Ruth and "Nino" took a trip to India together, and Ruth liked to show the picture of them riding a "magnificent, very elegant elephant." When her women friends asked why Scalia got to sit up front—because he was a man?—she said, dryly referring to how much larger her friend was, "It had to do with the distribution of weight."

Even the clerks were mystified by the relationship. But the clerks work at the court for a year—for the justices, this is life.

HOW RBG OPERATES

RBG depends on her clerks. She works them hard, but also rewards them with loyalty and generosity.

She shows great, almost motherly affection for them. She invites them to the opera and, while Marty was still alive, to her apartment to experience his cooking. She loves to know about their family life, and if they're single, who they're dating. She has performed wedding ceremonies for several of them. When they have children, she sends them "RBG grandclerk" T-shirts with the SCOTUS seal.

The most important job requirement is that clerks treat her two secretaries well. In Ruth's view, the secretaries are the people who keep the office running. She hates it when applicants treat her secretaries with disdain: "They are not hired help. As I tell my clerks, 'if push came to shove, I could do your work—but I can't do without my secretaries.'"

One of her very favorite clerks had been a stay-at-home dad for several years. "I was so pleased," she said, "to see that there are indeed men who are doing a parent's work, men who do not regard that as

RBG and Antonin Scalia riding an elephant in India in 1994

strange." It was a stance dear to her heart: "When fathers take equal responsibility for the care of their children, that's when women will truly be liberated." When the clerk's father was dying, the justice sent his parents a note saying how proud they should be of him.

Her clerks mostly set their own hours and get their instructions from RBG through voice mails she leaves at two or three in the morning. Yes, she remains a night owl, but doesn't expect others to follow her lead. If a clerk is working late and picks up the phone, she'll be startled: "What are you doing there?"

The court has an iron door that gets locked at two a.m. After that the SCOTUS police have to be called to let someone in and out—and RBG frequently makes that call.

A PERFECTIONIST

Ever since the days she studied with brilliant writer Vladimir Nabokov, RBG has placed great value on strong writing. The mantra in her chambers is "Get it right and keep it tight." A professor told her early on that her writing was a tad fancy, and she took a knife to adjectives after that: "If my opinion runs more than twenty pages," she said, "I am disturbed that I couldn't do it shorter." She hates to use the antiquated Latin terms often found in legalese—"If you can say it in plain English, you should"—and demands extra clarity in opening lines, which she writes herself and wants the public to be able to understand.

She and her clerks go through "innumerable drafts," with the goal of writing an opinion where no sentence needs to be read twice: "I think the law should be a literary profession, and the best legal practitioners regard law as an art as well as a craft."

A NEW FORMATION AT THE COURT

In 2005, Sandra Day O'Connor retired from the court at the relatively young age of seventy-five to take care of her ailing husband.

At former Chief Justice Rehnquist's funeral in 2005

Then Chief Justice Rehnquist died, leaving George W. Bush to fill two slots (with two men). Ruth had lost two cherished colleagues. The court was turning more conservative, intent on undoing or cutting back on what they saw as the court going too far in the 1960s and 1970s with its controversial rulings on abortion, segregated schools, public school prayers, the rights of defendants in criminal cases, and more.

Ruth hated being the only woman on the bench—"the word I

would use to describe my position on the bench is *lonely*." It brought back grim memories of standing out as strange and singular at law school. Once again women were a "one-at-a-time curiosity, not the normal thing" in a place of power. She believed the makeup of the court had damaging implications for all women. Girls wouldn't be able to imagine themselves on the court, and one woman couldn't possibly represent the diversity of all women.

In 2006 a journalist reminded Ruth that in her confirmation hearings she had said she expected to see three, four, or even more women on the court with her. "So where are they?" he asked—as if it were somehow her fault.

"Sadly they are not here," she replied. She went on, placing the blame elsewhere: "Because the president has not nominated them and the Senate has not confirmed another woman. You would have to ask the political leaders why a woman was not chosen."

It was as if history was moving backward. The number of female clerks had fallen to single digits for the first time in more than a decade. There were only seven women among the thirty-seven clerks, and two of them were working for Ruth.

A reporter asked her why this was the case, and Ruth said, "Why not ask a justice who has hired no women?"—of which there were four: Alito, Souter, Scalia, and Thomas.

SMOKING-HOT PEN, PART 2

All things considered, Ruth prefers to win.

But sometimes the strongest move she can make is to dissent, to dispute the court's majority opinion. It's a way to keep your dignity

and disagree. She tries everything to persuade others, but if she fails, it's time to let everyone know what she wishes had happened.

Over the years, Ruth has perfected her dissents, turning protest into an art form.

One night in the 1990s a woman named Lilly Ledbetter, a long-time area manager at the Goodyear Tire plant, found an anonymous note in her mailbox. It hadn't been easy working at the plant. One man had told her he took orders from a b— at home and wasn't about to take them from a b— at work. A boss had said she could improve her performance review by meeting up with him at a local motel. Nothing could have prepared her for what happened this time, though.

The piece of paper, from an unnamed friend trying to help her out, listed the salaries of all the tire-room managers. The men each made around $15,000 more than she did.

Lilly Ledbetter waited until she earned her retirement in 1998. Then she sued the company for discriminating against her, with her lawyers claiming that each paycheck was an act of discrimination. A federal appeals court ruled against her, saying that she had waited too long to sue. The next stop: the Supreme Court.

During oral arguments, Ledbetter studied Ruth, alone among the men on the bench: "We were around the same age, and she too had been one of the first women to break into her profession," she wrote later. "I might have been on the factory floor as she walked the hallowed halls of the American justice system, but I imagined that the men in ties and men in jeans can act just the same."

Ruth could have told her she was right about that.

In *Ledbetter v. Goodyear Tire & Rubber Co.*, the Supreme Court ruled against Ledbetter, saying that employees cannot sue for pay discrimination if it's more than 180 days after the onset of the discrimination, even if they didn't learn about the fact that they were being discriminated against until long after that 180 days had expired. To Ruth, this was unfair and ignored the reality of the working world.

She filed a vigorous dissent, of course. She tried to tell the male justices how clueless they were about what it was like to be a woman in the real world: "It's the story of almost every working woman of her generation, which is close to mine," she said later. "She is in a job that has been done by men until she comes along. She gets the job, and she's encountering all kinds of flak. But she doesn't want to rock the boat."

It was up to Ruth to rock it for her, with her blistering dissent.

THE GLOVES ARE OFF

People were noticing a new side to RBG. Right away the *New York Times* published an article with the headline "In Dissent, Ginsburg Finds Her Voice at Supreme Court." The idea that she had only just found her voice would come as a surprise to Marty, Ruth joked.

But her friends saw the change. "She has always been regarded as sort of a white-glove person," said one professor, "and she's achieved a lot that way. Now she is seeing that basic issues she's fought so hard for are in jeopardy, and she is less bound by what have been the conventions of the court."

Ruth declined to back down: "I will continue to give voice to my dissent if, in my judgment, the courts veers in the wrong direction where important matters are at stake."

In other words, the gloves were off.

Ruth was never one to draw attention to herself for no reason. Now, with her dissents, she was sending a signal that things were going very wrong: "Perhaps I am a little less tentative than when I was a new justice," she said. That was an understatement. "But what really changed was the composition of the court." In this atmosphere, her protests were more important than ever.

Her dissent in *Ledbetter* suggested that Congress could fix the law by clarifying that women like Ledbetter should have the chance to get their day in court. Two years later, the Lilly Ledbetter Fair Pay Act, signed by President Barack Obama in 2009, *reversed* the court's ruling.

This was the first bill he signed into law, with Lilly Ledbetter herself beaming behind him. The fact that it was President Obama's first priority gladdened Ruth's heart. She put a framed copy of the law, signed by the president as a birthday greeting, on her wall.

THE WORK GOES ON

In early 2009, Ruth suffered her second bout with cancer. The tumor in her pancreas was small and was caught early. Less than three weeks after surgery, she was back on the court, peppering lawyers with her usual pointed questions.

The next day she was taking her seat with the other justices at the first black president's inaugural speech to Congress. "Some of us were angry with her," said one clerk, "we kept telling her to slow down, we kept telling her to take it easy." He sent her novels to relax with, but "she wouldn't have any of it."

It was too important to her to represent women on the bench: "First I wanted people to see that the Supreme Court isn't all male." Plus she got a kick out of defying a senator who'd predicted that she was at death's door: "I also wanted them to see I was alive and well, contrary to that senator who said I'd be dead within nine months." (That senator died in 2017.)

Each Obama speech that Ruth attended featured a warm embrace between the two. "I've got a soft spot for Justice Ginsburg," said Obama, and Ruth agreed: "There was a rapport from the start between us."

BEING THIRTEEN YEARS OLD

Ruth, alas, was still the sole woman on the court when it came time to judge a sensitive case about a thirteen-year-old girl from Arizona.

Someone at school claimed that Savana Redding had given her prescription-strength ibuprofen, a drug that needs to be prescribed by a doctor. The school reacted by having Savana strip-searched for more drugs. Her outraged mother sued the school, and in spring of

2009 the case ended up at the Supreme Court as *Safford Unified School District v. Redding.*

How could strip-searching a kid be constitutional? It was a serious question, but some of the male justices seemed to find the whole case funny.

Justice Stephen Breyer rambled: "I'm trying to work out why this is a major thing to say strip down to your underclothes, which children do when they change for gym. In my experience when I was eight or ten or twelve years old, you know, we did take our clothes off once a day, we changed for gym, OK? And in my experience too, people did sometimes stick things in my underwear." Uncomfortable laughter stopped him for a moment.

But he pressed on: "Or not my underwear. Whatever. Whatever." More laughter. "I was the one who did it? I don't know. I mean, I don't think it's beyond human experience."

Ruth could take no more. "It wasn't just that they were stripped to their underwear," she retorted. "They were asked to shake their bra out—to shake, stretch the top of their pants, and shake that out."

After the oral argument, Ruth broke protocol by speaking outside of court about a case before the outcome was public. She fumed to a reporter about how the men on the court were completely out of touch: "They have never been a thirteen-year-old girl," she pointed out. "It's a very sensitive age for a girl. I don't think that my colleagues, some of them, quite understood."

RBG was tired of men not listening to her: "I don't know how many meetings I attended in the sixties and seventies, where I would say something, and I thought it was a pretty good idea," she told the

reporter. "Then someone else would say exactly what I said. Then people would become alert to it, respond to it."

And even at the Supreme Court, as a justice, it was still going on: "It can happen even in the conferences on the court. When I will say something—and I don't think I'm a confused speaker—and it isn't until somebody else says it that everyone will focus on the point."

ENTER SONIA

Then, in May of that year, President Barack Obama nominated distinguished Federal Appeals Court Judge Sonia Sotomayor to the Supreme Court. Ruth couldn't wait to welcome her. Since O'Connor had retired, Ruth had been stuck as the only woman on the court, and she was excited to be relieved of that role.

Sotomayor was the first Latina ever to be nominated. During her confirmation hearings, she was lambasted for a speech she had once given: "I wonder whether by ignoring our differences as women or men of color we do a disservice both to the law and society," she said, then went on, "Justice O'Connor has often been cited as saying a wise old man and wise old woman will reach the same conclusion in deciding cases. . . . I would hope that a wise Latina woman with the richness of her experiences would more often than not reach a better conclusion than a white male who hasn't lived that life."

Some senators pounced on her "wise Latina woman" speech, claiming that this woman who had grown up in a Bronx housing project was the real racist, and nearly derailing the nomination.

But Ruth understood what Sotomayor was saying: "I'm sure she meant no more than what I mean when I say: Yes, women bring a different life experience to the table. All of our differences make the conference better. That I'm a woman, that's part of it, that I'm Jewish, that's part of it, that I grew up in Brooklyn, New York, and I went to summer camp in the Adirondacks, all of these things are part of me."

Though affirmative action often got a bad name, Sotomayor bravely embraced it and its role in her life. She called herself a product of affirmative action. Ruth came to her side, saying, "So am I." It was a warm gesture of solidarity toward another woman who would represent a first for the Supreme Court.

After all the tumult, Sotomayor was confirmed, and in August she joined the Supreme Court.

Meanwhile, Ruth had finally been able to argue the men into seeing her point about eighth-grade student Savana.

On June 25, 2009, the court agreed with her, ruling that the school's strip-searching had been unconstitutional, a violation of Savana's rights.

Ruth took pride in changing her male colleagues' minds: "As we live, we can learn. It's important to listen. So I'm very glad that case came out as it did."

ENTER ELENA

When Elena Kagan was twelve years old, she did something Ruth wouldn't have dreamed of—she demanded that her rabbi give her a female version of a bar mitzvah, which was unheard of at her synagogue.

Obama's next nomination, in 2010, was this woman—Elena Kagan—meaning that for the first time three women sat on the bench at once. Ruth couldn't have been more elated.

As the first female dean of Harvard Law School, Kagan had recommended many clerks to Ruth. She was also the first woman to be confirmed as Solicitor General, the lawyer (or solicitor) who represents

the federal government in cases that go to the Supreme Court.

Kagan acknowledged that her path had been easier than Ruth's: "Female law firm partners and law school professors weren't exactly the norm, but their numbers were growing, and they weren't thought of as tokens or curiosities." She added, "Almost all federal judges and justices were happy to hire the brightest women as their clerks."

She continued, "Although I won't say I never felt any bias, it was pretty easy for me to pick the path of my choosing," and it was thanks to Ruth Bader Ginsburg: "More than any other person, she can take credit for making the law of this country work for women." Giving credit to the women who came before her was a very RBG thing to do.

The more women justices, the better, according to Ruth. People have repeatedly asked her when she thought there would be enough women on the court.

"When there are nine," she would say simply.

JUSTICE ELENA KAGAN

Appointed by Barack Obama
On the court since August 7, 2010
Kagan laughs that when she graduated from law
school, other judges on the D.C. Circuit offered her
clerkships, but "the only one of President Carter's
nominees to the D.C. Circuit who thought me not
quite good enough was Judge Ginsburg. She didn't
even interview me." This hasn't stopped them from
becoming close friends (or sharing a personal trainer).

JUSTICE ANTHONY KENNEDY

Appointed by Ronald Reagan
On the court since February 18, 1988
A fellow opera fan, Kennedy appeared
onstage in a Washington National Opera
production of *Die Fledermaus* along
with RBG and Breyer. On the bench, he
has sometimes annoyed her with his
patronizing opinions, but she was glad to
have him on her side in other cases, like
the same-sex marriage decisions.

JUSTICE SAMUEL ALITO

Appointed by George W. Bush
On the court since January 31, 2006
In 2013, Alito rolled his eyes and made faces
in the courtroom while RBG read a dissent
to his opinion. RBG was charitable: "It was
his natural reaction, but probably if he could
do it again, he would have squelched it." It
bothers her more that the ultraconservative
Alito replaced the moderate O'Connor.
"Every 5–4 decision when I was in the
minority, I would have been in the majority if
she'd stayed," RBG said in 2015.

JUSTICE SONIA SOTOMAYOR

Appointed by Barack Obama
On the court since August 8, 2009
When she was subjected to sexist
and bigoted criticism shortly after her
nomination, RBG spoke up on her behalf:
"The notion that Sonia is an aggressive
questioner—what else is new? Has
anybody watched Scalia or Breyer
on the bench?" RBG predicted
about Sonia, "She'll hold her own."

JUSTICE NEIL GORSUCH

Appointed by Donald Trump
On the court since April 7, 2017
While being questioned during his
confirmation hearings, Gorsuch
followed what's been called the
Ginsburg rule of "no hints, no
forecasts, no previews." Since then
she has commented, "I think he's very
easy to get along with. He writes very
well"—which is high praise indeed,
coming from RBG.

JUSTICE STEPHEN BREYER

Appointed by Bill Clinton
On the court since August 3, 1994
He tried to keep RBG awake at the
last State of the Union—he and
Kennedy "gave me a little jab, but
it wasn't enough."

CHIEF JUSTICE JOHN ROBERTS

Appointed by George W. Bush
On the court since September 29, 2005
A familiar face from his arguments before the
court, Roberts replaced Rehnquist, whom
RBG still sometimes calls "my chief." She
said in 2013, "I think the current chief is very
good at meeting and greeting people, always
saying the right thing in remarks he makes
for five or ten minutes at various gatherings."
She has said she hopes Roberts, like
Rehnquist, might be teachable on the issues
that matter to her.

JUSTICE CLARENCE THOMAS

Appointed by George H. W. Bush
On the court since October 23, 1991
Thomas calls RBG "a fabulous judge"
and a friend, but they're ideological
opposites. At his confirmation hearings,
law professor Anita Hill accused Thomas
of sexually harassing her. A copy of Hill's
book Race, Gender, and Power in America
has been spotted on RBG's bookshelf.

VOICES FOR, VOICES AGAINST

A SCOTUS anniversary for Ruth was coming up: fifteen years on the bench. Chief Justice John Roberts offered his "warm congratulations," adding that she had earned acclaim for her "work ethic, intellectual rigor, precision with words," not to mention her "total disregard for the normal day-night work schedule adhered to by everyone else since the beginning of recorded history." He was referring to her being a night owl.

Still, some people were calling on her to resign, to shuffle off to make way for President Obama to appoint someone younger during

the small window of time he had left. Despite a constant drumbeat in the background suggesting she step aside, Ruth had zero intention of retiring.

Friends who had seen older women pushed out of important positions before were furious at the pressure on Ruth. Said one: "She is a complete unique and wonderful gem on the court. There are so many cases, especially technical cases, where you read the majority and it doesn't seem all that bad. And then you read Ruth's dissent, and you realize they have just done something terrible."

THE IMPORTANCE OF MARTY

Meanwhile, Marty embraced his supporting role. His cooking delighted everyone. The Supreme Court Historical Society published a collection of his recipes, called *Chef Supreme*. Sometimes he made his own biscotti as treats for her clerks. On each clerk's birthday he would bake a cake—perhaps almond or chocolate, or ginger, lemon, or carrot.

"I was always in awe of her," said a former clerk, "but there was something disarming about seeing her with a partner who adores her but also treats her like a human being."

Another clerk remembered one late night, after an event, when Ruth was working in chambers while Marty read quietly nearby: "I started to talk to her about the research I had done, and while I was talking, Marty got up and walked toward us. I started freaking out in my mind—'Is what I am saying that stupid? What is he coming over here for?!'—only to watch him come up to RBG, fix her collar (which had somehow fallen into disarray), and then go back to his book. The comfortable intimacy of that moment was something I will always remember."

Marty was a member of a very small club made up of men married to powerful women, which he described as those whose wife has "a job which deep in your heart you wish you had." Then he added, "Now let me just say that in my case it isn't true. Only because I don't really like work. She works like fury all the time. The country's better off as it is."

Toward the end of his life, Marty got more serious. He told a friend, "I think that the most important thing I have done is enable Ruth to do what she has done."

He always had her back. When a writer described Ruth as "frail" in one of his books, Marty got in his face one day, asking, "How many push-ups can you do?"

The writer fumbled for an answer, and Marty retorted, "My wife can do twenty-five—and you wrote that she was frail!"

NEARLY SIXTY YEARS

The affection prevailed during the nearly sixty years of their marriage, surviving a total of three diagnoses of cancer.

But then cancer came back. In 2010, doctors said Marty had metastatic cancer.

"If my first memories are of Daddy cooking," their daughter Jane said, "so are my last. Cooking for Mother even when he could not himself eat, nor stand in the kitchen without pain, because for him it was ever a joy to discuss the law over dinner with Mother while ensuring that she ate well and with pleasure."

Before Marty's last trip to the hospital, Ruth found a letter that he had left for her on a yellow pad by the bed:

My dearest Ruth—You are the only person I have loved in my life, setting aside, a bit, parents and kids and their kids, and I have admired and loved you almost since the day we first met at Cornell some 56 years ago. What a treat it has been to watch you progress to the very top of the legal world!! I will be in JH Medical Center until Friday, June 25, I believe, and between then and now I shall think hard on my remaining health and life, and whether on balance the time has come for me to tough it out or to take leave of life because the loss of quality now simply overwhelms. I hope you will support where I come out, but I understand you may not. I will not love you a jot less. Marty.

6/17/10

My dearest Ruth —

You are the only person I have loved in my life, setting aside, a bit, parents and kids and their kids, and I have admired and loved you almost since the day we first met at Cornell some 56 years ago.

nearly 60

What a treat it has been to watch you progress to the very top of the legal world!!

I will be in FH medical center until Friday, June 25, I believe, and between then and now I shall think hard on my remaining health and life, and whether on balance the time has come for me to tough it out or to take leave of life because the loss of quality now simply overwhelms. I hope you will support where I come out, but I understand you may not. I will not love you a jot less.

Marty

He died on June 27. It happened to be the most important time of the Supreme Court calendar, the end of the term when all the big decisions come down. The court was actually in session the day after Marty's death, and Ruth was to give an opinion in a key case, about a Christian group at a public university trying to bar gay students from attending meetings.

She was famous for never missing a day, and that day would be no different. "My father would certainly not have wanted her to miss the last days on the bench on account of his death," said Jane.

That morning, as Chief Justice Roberts read a brief tribute to Marty, Ruth's good friend Scalia wept, while she sat there, very still, a dark ribbon in her hair.

Marty was buried in Arlington National Cemetery. Not long afterward, the folded American flag from his burial rested on the windowsill of Ruth's chambers.

The party the justices had to celebrate the end of the term was normally pretty tame. That year, however, peppy new Justice Sonia Sotomayor surprised everyone by putting on salsa music and cajoling the justices to dance with her. Ruth, in mourning, sat quietly on the side.

Sotomayor asked her to dance, whispering that Marty would have wanted her to. Ruth relented and danced a few steps, then held Sotomayor's face in her palms, murmuring, "Thank you."

RAISING HER VOICE

Some people thought Ruth wouldn't be able to go on after Marty's death, but they couldn't have been more wrong. Ruth forged ahead, doing the work, pulling all-nighters when she had to, dissenting away.

In 2010, one case especially perturbed her. It asked the question: How much can the government regulate corporate spending in elections? The answer, according to the court in *Citizens United v. Federal Election Commission*, was not much. It ruled that corporations and organizations can spend as much money as they want to help political candidates win elections.

Ruth was appalled. As one of the strongest voices against the corrupting influence of money in politics, she joined the dissent in that case, declaring later, "I think the notion that we have all the democracy that money can buy strays so far from what our democracy is supposed to be."

She felt so strongly that she eventually declared, "If there was one decision I would overrule, it would be *Citizens United*." Ruth was a powerful Supreme Court justice, but she didn't rule the world.

Another case the following year infuriated her. Female Walmart workers were bringing a class action suit against the company for pay discrimination. In *Walmart Stores, Inc. v. Dukes* (2011), the court ruled that the class action suit couldn't proceed because the women didn't have enough in common to constitute a class. Ruth's dissent sizzled: "The plaintiffs' evidence, including class members' tales of their own experiences, suggests that gender bias suffused Walmart's company culture," she observed.

If she were queen, the court would have made a different decision.

But that's just how the Supreme Court works. There are eight other strong-minded justices in the SCOTUS mix, and if Ruth is writing the majority opinion, she needs to keep at least four of them on her team.

After she circulates an opinion she has written, she has said, she will sometimes get notes saying, "Dear Ruth, I might join your opinion if you change this, that, or the other thing." Ruth tries to accommodate them, even when the end result isn't *exactly* what she would have wanted. On some cases, where the result may be close, her goal is keeping the liberal justices together and finding a way to get a fifth or even sixth vote.

RBG, as the longest serving among the more liberal justices, often assigns who writes the dissents: "I try to be fair, so no one ends up with all the dull cases while another has all the exciting cases. I do take I suppose more than a fair share of the dissenting opinions in the most-watched cases."

A dissenter's draft might be so persuasive that it wins a majority by flipping a vote or more—Ruth was able to pull that off once and called it "a heady experience."

FiVE IN oNE YEAR

The year of 2013 was her most spectacular yet: five dissents from the bench in all (breaking a half-century-long record among the justices). Ruth really did try to follow her mom's advice (getting angry was a waste of your own time), as well as her mother-in-law's (it sometimes helps to be a little deaf).

But she was growing weary of pretending not to hear. Within a few short years, decisions were threatening the progress for which she had fought so hard.

Some of her conservative colleagues were growing impatient with her dissents. As she read one aloud, Justice Samuel Alito rolled his eyes and shook his head, which was unheard-of disrespect at the court.

She didn't let it stop her.

RBG Takes a Passionate Stand

Woke up like this

flawless.

Supreme Court steps

flawless.

Alito stepping—

flawless.

writing a dissent

flawless.

A Beyoncé-inspired comic strip by Colleen Frakes

Courtroom sketch of RBG delivering her fiery dissent in the *Shelby* case on June 25, 2013, beside Justice Samuel Alito.

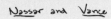

Cartoon by Hallie Jay Pope comically depicting four of RBG's dissents, notably in the *Shelby* case, with a resounding "NO" to Roberts's implication that racism is over.

The Dramatic Changes in Life Since the 1800s

★ 1855: A Missouri court rules that a black woman is the property of her master, without a right to defend herself against rape.

★ 1896: The National Association of Colored Women is founded to counter the racism in the suffrage movement; not until the 1960s were African American women able to freely exercise their right to vote in some Southern states.

★ 1918: The first women lawyers are admitted to the American Bar Association.

★ 1963: The Equal Pay Act makes it illegal for companies to pay different amounts to women and men for doing the same work.

★ 1964: As part of the Civil Rights Act, labeling want ads as jobs for men or women is made illegal.

★ 1972: Shirley Chisholm becomes the first African American woman to run for president.

★ 1973: Title IX of the Education Amendments bans sex discrimination in any federally funded school activities, like sports.

★ 1974: The Equal Credit Opportunity Act makes it illegal to refuse a credit card to a woman based on her gender.

★ 1974: The Women's Educational Equity Act is introduced by Representative Patsy Mink (the first Asian American woman elected to Congress) for the development of nonsexist teaching materials and programs that encourage full educational opportunities for girls and women.

★ 1975: Women are permitted to enroll in US military academies for the first time.

★ 1978: Women begin training to be astronauts.

★ 1978: According to the Pregnancy Discrimination Act, women can no longer be fired from their workplace for being pregnant.

★ 1979: Women's jury service becomes mandatory in all fifty states.

★ 1980: The Equal Employment Opportunity Commission formally defines sexual harassment on the job.

★ 1981: The Supreme Court overturns state laws designating a husband "head and master" with sole control of property owned jointly with his wife.

★ 1987: The Supreme Court rules that it is permissible to take sex and race into account in employment decisions even where there is no history of discrimination but when evidence of an imbalance exists in the number of women or minorities holding the position.

★ 1993: Women are allowed to wear pants on the US Senate floor.

★ 2013: The ban on women serving in combat in the military is lifted.

9

How to Become Notorious

THE DISSENTS KEEP COMING

RBG was in no mood to slow down. Take one particular case in 2014.

This case was dramatic, pitting religious beliefs against a woman's legal right to birth control. The owners of the Hobby Lobby chain of craft stores didn't want their medical insurance plans for employees to include certain forms of birth control, which they claimed violated their religious beliefs. With *Burwell v. Hobby Lobby*, the majority of the court agreed. In a controversial ruling, it said that family-run businesses can claim a religious exemption from laws if the laws contradict the owners' religious beliefs.

RBG vehemently dissented, declaring, "The court, I fear, has ventured into a minefield." She explained that she was all for respecting religious beliefs, but not if it harmed other people, like the nonreligious employees at Hobby Lobby who could not afford birth control.

Afterward, a reporter asked her, "Do you believe that the five male justices truly understood the ramifications of their decision?"

Ruth, whose two fellow female justices had joined her dissent, along with Justice Breyer, replied, "I would have to say no."

Did they, as men, show a blind spot?

They certainly did, said RBG: "Contraceptive protection is something every woman must have access to, to control her own destiny. I certainly respect the belief of the Hobby Lobby owners. On the other hand, they have no constitutional rights to foist that belief on the hundreds and hundreds of women who work for them who don't share that belief."

The case seemed to be a serious step backward for women.

GETTING HER OWN WAY

James Obergefell had a lot in common with some of Ruth's clients from her lawyer days. By the time he came to the Supreme Court, he was a widower who had cared for his partner, demanding the court fix an unfair law. When his partner, John Arthur, had gotten incurably sick in 2011, the two had traveled to another state to be married, but Ohio, where they lived, said their marriage wasn't valid because they were two men. He went to court, saying Ohio's law was unconstitutional.

By this point RBG had performed two same-sex wedding ceremonies, the first justice to do so. She said: "People who love each other and want to live together should be able to enjoy the blessings and the strife in the marriage relationship." (The good, the bad, and the ugly.)

At court that day, one of the lawyers arguing against state laws that refused to recognize same-sex marriage had a secret: underneath his proper button-down shirt, he wore a "NOTORIOUS R.B.G." T-shirt.

Justice [Ginsburg] [with opinion] in Wood v. Moss, 5-27-14

Lawyers for the states defending their laws argued that same-sex couples could not be let into marriage because the institution was rooted in thousands of years of tradition.

RBG cut in, "There was a change in the institution of marriage to make it egalitarian when it wasn't egalitarian"—more equal. "Same-sex unions wouldn't fit into what marriage once was"—a tradition that saw women as property. She was an expert on this, having herself helped remake marriage, freeing it from the laws limiting roles for men and women.

Another justice, Anthony Kennedy, was almost always the tie-breaking vote, and he wrote the majority opinion striking down bans on same-sex marriage.

But it was RBG's image, rendered in rainbow colors, roaring on a motorcycle across the steps of the Supreme Court, that dominated the celebrations following the victory.

A RUTHLESS EDITOR

Ruth usually assigns her clerks to write the first draft of an opinion. They give it their very best shot, then brace themselves for a brutal edit.

One clerk remembered a draft where RBG had crossed out and re-written every single word in one paragraph—except "the," which she'd circled in a move the clerk assumed was meant as a compliment.

Ruth edits even minor punctuation in the draft of a speech that is only going to be spoken, never published. A rumor lingers that she once sent a letter in reply to an applicant for clerkship who made a typo in her application: "Note the typo." (The candidate was not interviewed.)

At the end of one term, her clerks presented her with the gift of a menu, edited in her fashion—nearly every word changed.

One clerk got the ultimate compliment when he handed in a draft: "Marty wanted me to go to a movie and I said no," she said, having set aside her whole evening to redo the draft. "But this is so good I'm going to the movies."

Grammar is important, but so is tone. She always wants to treat the losing side respectfully: "My writing style tends to be, some people might think, more bland. I'm not as immediately attention-grabbing, but I hope that what I write has staying power." Her approach differed from that of Scalia, who hurled "irrational," "utter nonsense," "pure applesauce," and "it should be destroyed" at opinions he disagreed with. She prefers to quote Learned Hand (the judge who refused to hire her because he wanted to be able to curse freely) that you shouldn't knock your opponent's chess pieces off the table.

For the losers, said a clerk describing Ruth's instructions to them, "The important takeaway for them is not just 'I lost.' It should be 'I was treated fairly and understand the judiciary.'" As an extra sign of respect, RBG even instructs her clerks not to use the "courts below" or "lower courts" to describe the district and appeals courts.

"AWESOMELY GOOD"

Even with all this perfectionism, RBG is famous for getting opinions done in a timely manner. "We all laugh about how fast she is," marveled Elena Kagan. "And her work is just awesomely good. In my book she is the consummate judicial craftsman, and I learn something from her every time we sit."

When RBG needs an in-person consult, she uses a buzzer to summon clerks to her inner sanctum. Clerks have learned to adjust to what several of them called "her tolerance for conversational silence." She chooses her spoken words as carefully as the words she writes. "There are no words that are not preceded by thoughts," said a friend.

"I'm gon' call my crew"

How do you know when Ruth is done speaking? One clerk described his tactic: "There was always a point where you thought you were at the end of the conversation where you weren't sure if she was fully done. You would slowly start backing up towards the door, and if she said something you'd come back, and if she didn't say anything you'd continue out the door."

Another clerk said he applied the "five Mississippi" rule to the silence. After that long of a pause, it was safe to leave.

TOUGH AS NAILS

So how does RBG stay in fighting shape—lifting those heavy law books, keeping lawyers on their toes, and hurling those flaming dissents, all on little sleep?

Besides her fondness for the most active of sports—horseback riding, water-skiing, whitewater rafting, and more—she works out with vigor.

Defying the stereotype of a dainty lady, she sought adventure and strenuous activity whenever she had the chance. While spending a week in residence at the University of Hawaii in 1998, for example, she took great pleasure in joining a students' kayak crew. While whitewater rafting on the Colorado River, she was told to sit in the back of the boat so if it hit a rock she wouldn't go flying off.

Her response: "I don't sit in the back."

Ruth keeps herself fit by making good use of the justices' gym. She worked out to classical music until a TV was installed. PBS's *NewsHour* was her preferred viewing. She tried a Jazzercise class, but found the "loud music . . . quite awful."

She's had the same personal trainer for the last two decades, meeting up twice a week, usually after she leaves the office at seven p.m. Bryant Johnson is a buff army-reserve sergeant who was deployed in Kuwait. Impressive professional women are his speciality—"I have been raised with a lot of strong women in my life that help influence

Whitewater rafting in Colorado in 1990

how I look at women, which is as equal to a man"—but RBG is the one he calls TAN, for "tough as nails."

In the first few months he worked with her, he was worried that he hadn't gotten any feedback from her. One of her secretaries let him in on a secret: "If the justice didn't like you, you wouldn't still be here."

With Ruth, Johnson concentrates on strength training—stretching exercises, lifting weights, various kinds of push-ups. She never complains.

He likes to joke around with her—she actually laughs—and rarely does he cut her any slack, except for the day she came in with a cracked rib and he had to hold her back.

Their sessions are a high priority for RBG. In fact, she once slipped out early from a White House dinner with Obama—intent on keeping her appointment at the gym.

"I said, 'You left the president for me?'" Johnson recalled. "Oh man, extra push-ups for you."

At Barack Obama's first speech to Congress in 2009

RBG's Exercise Routine, Part 2

⭐ five-minute warm-up on the elliptical

⭐ stretching and rotational exercises

⭐ one-legged squats

⭐ planks

Bryant Johnson's five-point signature move

1. Sit down on a bench with a twelve-pound ball. (You can start with a two-pound ball and work your way up.)

2. Stand up, holding the ball with two hands pressed to your chest.

3. Toss it to Johnson, who hands it back. ("I don't want to take the chance she misses it and it hits her. That wouldn't be a good look. Just think of the paperwork I would have to fill out.")

4. Sit back down on the bench.

5. Repeat ten times.

10

Reason to Hope that We Will See a Better Day

*R*uth's chambers, except for the pencils covering the black granite desk, show off her good taste in all things. Favorite paintings on the walls uplift her. One of the job's perks is getting to borrow artwork from Washington's famed museum collections, and she takes full advantage. Her favorite artist is Henri Matisse, but she likes many other, more obscure artists, like the American abstract artist Ben Cunningham. She has borrowed paintings by the modern abstract painters Mark Rothko, Max Weber, and Josef Albers.

In her chambers in 2002

DAILY LIFE

RBG's daughter, Jane, has gone on to be a distinguished professor at Columbia Law School (making her and Ruth the first-ever mother-daughter professor pair at the school). Her son, James, attended the University of Chicago, dutifully starting out in law but turning to his real love: music. He is the founder of Cedille Records, a classical label that launched while he was still a student.

Jane comes down to Washington, D.C., from New York and spends the weekends cooking for her mom. In the freezer she leaves behind little packages of meals marked "chicken" or "fish."

RBG still spends the weekends catching up on sleep that she

misses during the week. "Sometimes she'll be going to sleep just as I'm waking up," said Jane. Marty was the one who always told Ruth to get some rest, that solutions would be clearer in the morning. "But

now there's no one telling me it's time to quit," RBG mourns.

When court is in session, the US marshals make sure she is supplied with caffeine. "She lives off coffee," said her granddaughter Clara, who stayed with Ruth for a summer.

She is as fierce as ever. She strives "to seek ever more the joys of being alive, because who knows how much longer I will be living? At my age, one must take things day by day."

THE WORK GOES ON

Over the course of the centuries, according to RBG, people left out of the Constitution fought to have their humanity recognized by it. She has seen that struggle as her life's work.

RBG Speaks

"I think gender discrimination is bad for everyone, it's bad for men, it's bad for children. Having the opportunity to be part of that change is tremendously satisfying. Think of how the Constitution begins. 'We the people of the United States in order to form a more perfect union.' But we're still striving for that more perfect union. And one of the perfections is for the 'we the people' to include an ever enlarged group."

RBG is committed to keeping conversation civil at court, but she's also committed to calling out sexism in the workplace, even her own. When asked if she still experienced sexism, she instantly said, "Yes. Less than I once did. Once it happened all the time that I would say something and there was no response. And then a man would say the same thing and people would say 'good idea!'" With a laugh, she added, "That happens much less today."

Her response to sexism, she says, is to "try to teach through my opinions, through my speeches, how wrong it is to judge people on the basis of what they look like, color of their skin, whether they're men or women."

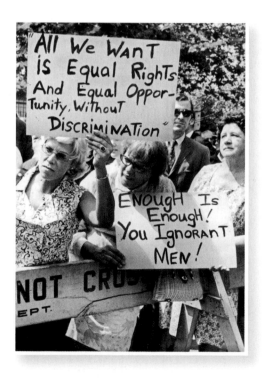

When her friend Antonin Scalia died in 2016, she didn't just lose a colleague. "We were best buddies," she mourned.

It also created a gap on the court. SCOTUS needs nine justices to function properly—someone has to be a tiebreaker.

Obama, in his last year as president, nominated Merrick Garland, a respected moderate judge, to replace Scalia. His Republican opponents took the unprecedented path of refusing to even hold a hearing for Garland. They said it wouldn't be right to consider a new justice

during an election year—a rule that technically has no basis in either history or the Constitution. So the Supreme Court had to carry on making decisions with eight votes (four fairly liberal, four fairly conservative) instead of nine—no tiebreaker. In the handful of cases with a 4–4 vote, the lower court's opinion stood.

RBG was hopeful about the 2016 election. "Wouldn't that be fantastic?" was her reaction to the prospect of our first woman president, Hillary Clinton.

But it was not to be. After businessman Donald Trump's election, he began undoing much of what Obama had accomplished. In Trump's third month in office, he signed a bill revoking Obama's Fair Pay and Safe Workplaces executive order, one of the ways Obama had tried to fight wage discrimination.

In 2017, he appointed Court of Appeals Judge Neil Gorsuch to replace Scalia, and he may have the opportunity to appoint other new justices, ones that agree with him.

While keeping herself in supreme fighting shape, RBG strives to maintain her balance and her optimism: "We are not experiencing the best of times, but there is reason to hope that we will see a better day," she said in 2017.

Back in 2011, she teasingly said she wouldn't retire at least until she got her favorite Josef Albers painting back from a traveling exhibition in 2012. The day came and went.

She still has no plans to retire. "When I forget the names of cases that I could once recite at the drop of a hat," she says, "I will know."

She hates being told to slow down.

Acknowledgments

The authors are grateful to Aubri Juhasz for rigorous fact-checking assistance. Warm thanks, too, to Linda Loewenthal and Lindsay Edgecombe, and to the entire team at HarperCollins Children's Books.

Legal Terms
in Plain English

affirmative action A program, particularly in education or employment, intended to fix historical injustice, favoring groups that have been discriminated against in the past.

American Civil Liberties Union (ACLU) A nonprofit national organization, with branches in almost all states, that takes legal action "to defend and preserve the individual rights and liberties guaranteed to every person in this country by the Constitution and laws of the United States."

appeal A request to a higher court to reverse a decision by a lower court.

brief A written argument presented in court to argue for one side of a case.

Constitution The supreme law of the United States, listing how the American government is to be administered.

constitutional A law or ruling in agreement with principles in the American Constitution.

counsel Another word for lawyer, or advice coming from a lawyer.

court of appeals Also known as appellate court—a court that determines whether or not the law has been applied correctly in a lower court.

dissent A disagreement with a ruling by the other judges, disputing the court's majority opinion.

Fourteenth Amendment The amendment to the Constitution that covers citizens' right to equal protection of the law.

judge Someone who presides over court proceedings, conducting a trial impartially and issuing rulings either alone or as part of a panel.

law review A scholarly journal focusing on legal matters, usually published through a law school.

lawyer/attorney A person who practices the law, performing legal services and applying laws to specific cases.

opinion A judge's decision on a legal matter.

oral argument A presentation spoken aloud in court of why a lawyer's reasoning should prevail, during which judges and justices may ask questions.

plaintiffs Those who bring a case against others in court, starting a lawsuit.

precedent An earlier decision by a court to be used as a guide in future decisions.

recuse When judges excuse themselves from deciding a case because of the possibility they can't be impartial.

Solicitor General The lawyer representing the United States government in arguing cases before the Supreme Court.

Supreme Court The highest court of the United States, the final interpreter of the law according to the Constitution.

unconstitutional A law or ruling that violates a principle in the American Constitution.

v. Used in names of court cases for *versus*, a Latin word meaning against.

Sources

Abramson, Jill. "Class of Distinction: Women Find Success After Harvard Law '59, Despite the Difficulties—Judge Ginsburg's Classmates Balanced Lives, Careers, Helped Shape Profession—'Ecstatic' Over Appointment." *Wall Street Journal*, July 20, 1993.

Association of American Law Schools. "Engendering Equality: A Conversation with Justice Ginsburg." YouTube.com, February 20, 2015.

Barnes, Robert. "The Question Facing Ruth Bader Ginsburg: Stay or Go?" *Washington Post*, October 4, 2013.

Bazelon, Emily. "The Place of Women on the Court." *New York Times*, July 7, 2009.

Biskupic, Joan. "Ginsburg: Court Needs Another Woman." *USA Today*, October 5, 2009.

———. "Ginsburg 'Lonely' Without O'Connor; The Remaining Female Justice Fears Message Sent by Court Composition." *USA Today*, January 25, 2007.

———. "Ginsburg, Scalia Strike a Balance." *USA Today*, December 25, 2007.

———. "Justice Ginsburg Reflects on Term, Leadership Role." *USA Today*, June 30, 2011.

Carlson, Margaret. "The Law According to Ruth." *Time*, June 24, 2001.

Carmon, Irin. "Ruth Bader Ginsburg on Marriage, Sexism, and Pushups." MSNBC, February 17, 2015.

Davidson, Kenneth M., Ruth Bader Ginsburg, and Herma Hill Kay. *Sex-Based Dis-*

crimination: Text, Cases and Materials. Eagan, MN: West Publishing Company, 1974.

Dodson, Scott, ed. *The Legacy of Ruth Bader Ginsburg.* Cambridge: Cambridge University Press, 2015.

Epstein, Nadine. "Ruth Bader Ginsburg: 'The Notorious RBG.'" *Moment Magazine,* May 2015.

Feigen, Brenda. *Not One of the Boys: Living Life as a Feminist.* New York: Knopf, 2000.

Gilbert, Lynn. *Particular Passions: Ruth Bader Ginsburg.* New York: Lynn Gilbert Inc., 2012.

Ginsburg, Ruth Bader. "The Changing Complexion of Harvard Law School." *Harvard Women's Law Journal* 27 (2004): 303, 305.

———. "A Conversation with Associate Justice Ruth Bader Ginsburg." *Columbia University Law Review* 84 (2013): 909, 929.

———. "Distinguished Lecture on Women and the Law." C-SPAN, February 3, 2014.

———. "From Brooklyn to the Bench." Cornell University, September 22, 2014.

———. Interview. Academy of Achievement: A Museum of Living History, August 17, 2010.

———. Keynote Speech at Harvard Law School Celebration, Cambridge, MA, April 15, 1978.

———. MAKERS Video Collection of Women's Stories, February 26, 2013, www.makers.com/ruth-bader-ginsburg.

———. "On Hobby Lobby, *Roe v. Wade*, Retirement and Notorious R.B.G." Yahoo News Video, July 31, 2014.

———. Prospectus for the Women's Rights Project of the American Civil Liberties Union. 1972.

———. Remarks for American Bar Association Initiative: "Renaissance of Idealism in the Legal Profession." May 2, 2006.

———. Remarks at Columbia Law School, New York City, May 1980.

———. Remarks for George Mason University School of Law Graduation. *George Mason Independent Law Review* 1 (1993).

———. Remarks at Georgetown University Law Center. C-SPAN, February 4, 2015.

———. Remarks at Hawaii Women Lawyers' Tea, October 30, 1986.

———. Remarks for Rutgers School of Law–Newark, April 11, 1995.

———. Remarks on Women's Progress in the Legal Profession in the United States.

Tulsa Law Review 33 (1997): 13, 15.

———. "The Role of Dissenting Opinions." *Minnesota Law Review* 95 *(*2010): 1.

———. "The Supreme Court: A Place for Women." *Vital Speeches of the Day*, May 1, 2001.

———. "A Woman's Voice May Do Some Good." *Politico*, September 25, 2013.

———. Justice Ginsburg Speaks: "Women and the Law; Syria, Congress and the President and More." *The Takeaway with John Hockenberry*, September 16, 2013.

Ginsburg, Ruth Bader, and Dorit Beinisch. Interview by Nina Totenberg. 92Y Plus, YouTube.com, October 22, 2014.

Goldberg, Stephanie B. "The Second Woman Justice." *ABA Journal*, October 1993, 42.

Greenburg, Jan Crawford. *Supreme Conflict: The Inside Story of the Struggle for Control of the United States Supreme Court.* New York: Penguin, 2007.

Greenhouse, Linda. "Oral Dissents Give Ginsburg a New Voice." *New York Times*, May 31, 2007.

———. "Word for Word: A Talk with Ginsburg on Life and the Court." *New York Times*, January 7, 1994.

Gunther, Gerald. "Ruth Bader Ginsburg: A Personal, Very Fond Tribute." *University of Hawai'i Law Review* 20 (1998): 583, 586.

Hamilton, Mildred. "Ruth Wins One for ERA." *New Jersey Examiner*, March 24, 1975.

"High Court Outlaws Sex Discrimination." *New York Post*, November 22, 1971.

Hope, Judith Richards. *Pinstripes and Pearls: The Women of the Harvard Law Class of '64 Who Forged an Old Girl Network and Paved the Way for Future Generations.* New York: Scribner, 2008.

Josephson, Larry. "A Conversation with Justice Ruth Bader Ginsburg: Her Life as a Woman, a Jew and a Judge." *Only in America*, September 2, 2004.

Kashino, Marisa M. "Stage Presence: Ruth Bader Ginsburg's Love of the Arts." *Washingtonian*, October 10, 2012.

Kerber, Linda K. *No Constitutional Right to Be Ladies: Women and the Obligations of Citizenship.* New York: Hill & Wang, 1998.

Labaton, Stephen. "The Man Behind the High Court Nominee." *New York Times*, June 17, 1993.

Lamb, Brian, Susan Swain, and Mark Farkas, eds. *The Supreme Court: C-SPAN Book Featuring the Justices in Their Own Words.* New York: PublicAffairs, 2010.

Lapham, Lewis H. "Old Masters at the Top of Their Game." *New York Times Magazine*, October 23, 2014.

Ledbetter, Lilly. *Grace and Grit: My Fight for Equal Pay and Fairness at Goodyear and Beyond*. New York: Three Rivers Press, 2013.

Lewis, Neil A. "Rejected as a Clerk, Chosen as a Justice." *New York Times*, June 15, 1993.

Liptak, Adam. "Court Is 'One of the Most Activist,' Ginsburg Says, Vowing to Stay." *New York Times*, August 24, 2013.

———. "Kagan Says Path to Supreme Court Was Made Smoother Because of Ginsburg's." *New York Times*, February 10, 2014.

———. "Right Divided, a Disciplined Left Steered the Supreme Court." *New York Times*, June 30, 2015.

Margolick, David. "Trial by Adversity Shapes Jurist's Outlook." *New York Times*, June 25, 1993.

Mathews, Jay. "The Spouse of Ruth: Marty Ginsburg, the Pre-Feminism Feminist." *Washington Post*, June 19, 1993.

Oelsner, Lesley. "Columbia Law Snares a Prize in the Quest for Women Professors." *New York Times*, January 26, 1972.

Ostrer, Mitchel. "Columbia's Gem of the Motion: A Profile of Ruth Bader Ginsburg." *Juris Doctor*, October 1977.

Page, Clarence. "President Clinton's 'Stealth' Justice." *Chicago Tribune*, June 20, 1993.

Peppers, Todd C., and Artemus Ward. *In Chambers: Stories of Supreme Court Law Clerks and Their Justices*. Charlottesville: University of Virginia Press, 2012.

Pogrebin, Abigail. *Stars of David: Prominent Jews Talk About Being Jewish*. New York: Random House, 2007.

Pullman, Sandra. *Tribute: The Legacy of Ruth Bader Ginsburg and WRP Staff*. ACLU, February 19, 2006, www.aclu.org/other/tribute-legacy-ruth-bader-ginsburg-and-wrp-staff.

Rosen, Jeffrey. "The Book of Ruth." *New Republic*, August 2, 1993.

———. "The New Look of Liberalism on the Court." *New York Times*, October 5, 1997.

———. "Ruth Bader Ginsburg Is an American Hero." *New Republic*, September 28, 2014.

Saulnier, Beth. "Justice Prevails: A Conversation with Ruth Bader Ginsburg '54." *Cornell Alumni Magazine*, November/December, 2013.

Supreme Court Opinion Announcements, oyez.org.

The Supreme Court of the United States Blog, SCOTUSblog.

Strebeigh, Fred. *Equal: Women Reshape American Law*. New York: Norton, 2009.

Swiger, Elinor Porter. *Women Lawyers at Work*. New York: Messner, 1978.

Symposium Honoring the 40th Anniversary of Justice Ruth Bader Ginsburg Joining the Columbia Law Faculty: A Conversation with Justice Ginsburg, Columbia Law School, February 10, 2012.

Thomas, Marlo, ed. *The Right Words at the Right Time*. New York: Atria, 2004.

Toobin, Jeffrey. "Heavyweight." *New Yorker*, March 11, 2013.

———. *The Nine: Inside the Secret World of the Supreme Court*. New York: Doubleday, 2007.

———. *The Oath: The Obama White House and the Supreme Court*. New York: Doubleday, 2012.

Traister, Rebecca. "How Ruth Bader Ginsburg Became the Most Popular Woman on the Internet." *New Republic*, July 10, 2014.

Von Drehle, David. "Conventional Roles Hid a Revolutionary Intellect." *Washington Post*, July 18, 1993.

Vrato, Elizabeth. *The Counselors: Conversations with 18 Courageous Women Who Have Changed the World*. Philadelphia: Running Press, 2002.

Weiden, David L., and Artemus Ward. *Sorcerers' Apprentices: 100 Years of Law Clerks at the United States Supreme Court*. New York: NYU Press, 2006.

Weinstock, Sue. "Robes for Two Ladies." *Newark Star-Ledger*, June 4, 1970.

Weisberg, Jessica. "Supreme Court Justice Ruth Bader Ginsburg: I'm Not Going Anywhere." *Elle*, September 23, 2014.

Williams, Susan H., and David C. Williams. "Sense and Sensibility: Justice Ruth Bader Ginsburg's Mentoring Style as a Blend of Rigor and Compassion." *University of Hawai'i Law Review* 20 (1998): 589.

Wolf, Richard. "Ginsburg's Dedication Undimmed After 20 Years on Court." *USA Today*, August 1, 2013.

Also: Interviews with Ruth Bader Ginsburg, Jane Ginsburg, James Ginsberg, Gloria Steinem, Aminatou Sow, Frank Chi, Burt Neuborne, Judith Lichtman, Hesh Kaplan, Anita Fial, Brenda Feigen, Diane Zimmerman, David Schizer, Lynn Hecht Schafran, Margo Schlanger, Paul Spera, Clara Spera, Dan Canon, Marcia Greenberger, Richard Primus, Daniel Rubens, Bryan Garner, Alisa Klein, Paul Berman, David Post, Scott Hershovitz, Cynthia Fuchs Epstein, and others.

Image Credits

Chapter 9: How to Become Notorious

Chapter 10: Reason to Hope that We Will See a Better Day

Acknowledgments

Legal Terms in Plain English

Index

Italicized page numbers indicate images.